I0711948

LOST AND LIVED IN

Michelle Ray Prellz

authorHOUSE®

AuthorHouse™
1663 Liberty Drive
Bloomington, IN 47403
www.authorhouse.com
Phone: 833-262-8899

Published by AuthorHouse 05/26/2023

ISBN: 979-8-8230-0831-0 (sc)
ISBN: 979-8-8230-0832-7 (hc)
ISBN: 979-8-8230-0830-3 (e)

Library of Congress Control Number: 2023908774

Print information available on the last page.

This book is printed on acid-free paper.

CONTENTS

Intro vii

Chapter 1   Before the Storm 1

Chapter 2   Foreshadowing 3

Chapter 3   Becoming Noticeable 7

Chapter 4   College 13

Chapter 5   Trigger Warning: Self Harm 19

Chapter 6   Trigger Warning: Eating Disorder Behaviors 23

Chapter 7   Resisting Treatment 28

Chapter 8   Treatment 31

Chapter 9   Unwilling 35

Chapter 10   Trying for the Wrong Reasons 40

Chapter 11   A Setback with Grandpa 43

Chapter 12   Trigger Warning: Alcoholism and Suicidal Ideation 46

Chapter 13   Navigating Suicidal Ideation 53

Chapter 14   Special Occasions 56

Chapter 15   Grandpa's Passing 60

Chapter 16   Trigger Warning: The Effects of my eating disorder 64

Chapter 17   Trigger Warning: Sexual Assault 67

Chapter 18   The Breaking Point 73

Chapter 19   Treatment- Take 2 78

Chapter 20   Values 84

Chapter 21   Trust 89

Chapter 22   The Intervention 93

Chapter 23   The Real Start 98

Chapter 24   Preparation 107

Chapter 25   Guilt 114

Chapter 26   Working Through the Trauma 118

Chapter 27 Disconnected 123
Chapter 28 All of the Moving Parts 126
Chapter 29 The Final Pieces 130
Chapter 30 We Forget How to Play 132
Chapter 31 Breaking the Seal 137
Chapter 32 Meant to Be 139
Chapter 33 Blessed 142

INTRO

I have always had this need to organize my headspace. If I could, I would have laid out all my thoughts, big and small, across the floor. Millions of them. And took the time to piece them together into a finished puzzle. I wanted to understand what I was going through and how to explain it to others. Mental illness was just a word. I wanted it to be tangible, more than a word. Something to grasp.

Writing was my way to make sense of it all. It was the platform in which I communicated this part of my life to family and friends. I could let people into my mind without having to speak it or be in the same place for that matter. They could take or leave what they wanted.

Once I started recovering, I could see more clearly how I got to my rock bottom, foreshadowing events, why I thought a certain way, why I did or didn't do certain things that me or no one else understood at the time, why I gave up and got worse. I can now identify what I needed in those moments, even though I didn't know in the midst of them.

This book is my first hand account of the wrath of mental illness. A tour inside my mind while I developed and lived with major depression, an eating disorder, anxiety/OCD, alcohol abuse, trauma and sexual assault. It's not going to make beautiful something that destroyed me and my loved ones. It's the completely raw, unfiltered journey that I walked for about ten years of my life. My thoughts and feelings before I knew something was wrong, during the darkest struggles, two times in treatment, and a recovery I wouldn't trade for anything. It's everything I learned throughout, and how I got to a place where I can maintain recovery.

It's dark, uncomfortable, and possibly heart breaking. But it's real. I wrote this in hopes that someone out there who is trying to understand for a struggling loved one can open this book and walk with me through the darkness to gain clarity, but also hope. I want to start much needed conversations and spark ideas around support.

I stopped trying to fight after so long. That lack of motivation bled into most other areas of my life. Rock bottom became my baseline. It took years to start fighting for myself again. I hope I can be a voice for those who aren't ready to ask for help or talk about it yet. Although no one else could save me from my mental illness, having people who held my hand while I saved myself was crucial.

Not everyone experiences mental illness in the same way, but unfortunately it's often a familiar darkness that we experience. The world will tell you someone has it way worse. You'll compare to the war stories others have, feeling like your story isn't deserving of repair. You'll get the idea that you have no reason to feel this way. The world will romanticize mental illness, putting you down for an uglier, less desirable story.

I was normal, untouchable. I lived a comfortable life with supportive family and my mind still broke me. Anyone and everyone can be effected by the wrath. It doesn't matter what kind of story you have. If it hurts, it hurts. Your pain is valid. Don't let society make you hide for fear of being real.

The story of how far someone has come is important to hear and celebrate, but I think a huge chunk of that story is often looked over. And that is acknowledging where it is we came so far from. To those listening, it's just words, a story that can be closed in between two covers and set on a shelf for later. A story that is heard but taken by the wind when the conversation is over. To those of us telling our story, it's more than a story, it's our life.

Ten plus years later, I started figuring out who I was, what I liked to do, who I wanted to surround myself with, and what I dreamed of for my future. Before healing, I lost myself. I never thought of a future for myself. My identity became defined only by my pain. In order to find myself, I needed to get better and experience the world through clear eyes. I had to live life without looking through the lens of my issues to know who I truly was. It was only then that I could be present in my own life. And what I found was a beautifully imperfect world, created by God, with a plan for me.

Everything leading up to the day I chose recovery is just as much my story as the good stuff. It's the standard I held my life to for so long. It's what I thought I deserved. The quiet struggles that are now just the beginning of my story when they could have been the end. So many of the blessings we receive in life grow from the storms that bury us. The struggles in life always get worse before they can get better. It's a messy fight, but it's so worth the fight.

Before the Storm

I don't like the concept of normal. It's a label that makes me think of sheltered, comfortable, even privileged. I don't know if normal actually exists in a world this diverse. Either anything at all or nothing at all is normal. I think we can all have our own definition of what we think it is, but each of our answers is relative to our personal view of the world.

I used to consider my life growing up normal. A nice kind of normal. I grew up with one brother and both parents in the home for much of my childhood. We lived in a normal sized house in a normal suburb of Columbus, Ohio. We went to a normal elementary school, and church on Sundays together. Our grandparents were a huge part of our lives as well.

My brother and I played outside with all our neighborhood friends every day until dark. Our yard was the headquarters where all the kids would come to play. A woman had told my mom once that she loved passing by our house because we were always up to something out there. Bikes and scooters littered the yard like fallen leaves. We ran around barefoot, played games we made up, and climbed trees. Our biggest worry was if Mom and Dad were going to make us take a bath that night.

Our parents provided us with all our basic needs, the average middle-class family. And although we weren't the type to ask for the nicest and latest things, there were a few times growing up that mom or dad would let us pick out a toy at the store when it wasn't even our birthday. We could eat out on weekends after church, and we never went hungry.

I sometimes wondered if the kids who couldn't afford a baby doll from the toy store, or maybe didn't have both parents were the normal ones and we were just lucky. In either case, it made me question how I could even claim that I got depressed with such a sound upbringing. Of course, things weren't perfect, but things were good. I should have turned out fine considering I was well taken care of.

I was ashamed when I started getting help. Not because of embarrassment or fear of judgment. It was because I felt undeserving. I was sitting in front of a therapist I was fortunate enough to have. It felt like a pity party, with no origin or reason. I didn't deserve to be worked on. There were people out there who were dealt a bad hand before they even had a chance. Those were the people who deserved help. I was dealt a good hand, but somehow screwed it up. That felt more like my own fault. I always thought a story like this would be better told by anyone else. The comeback story belonged to the one who started in a hole. Not someone like me who made something out of nothing.

Was I ungrateful? Was I blind to my blessings? Why did I feel so damaged? Normal felt like a place that couldn't be touched by depression. And because my normal was touched by it, did that count? Did my lack of circumstances discredit the pain I felt?

2

Foreshadowing

Other than a good home life, I had a good experience at my elementary school as well. I went to a large public school in my city. Just like any other kid, recess was my favorite. I was quiet in school, not shy, but the type to avoid attention. I never got in trouble, I did what I was supposed to do, and I got along with everyone.

The anxiety I started to feel in fifth grade wasn't far from the usual stuff. Touring the sixth grade building was intimidating, too many hallways, lockers everywhere, splitting up for classes instead of stating with one class. That stuff was nerve racking to all of us. I imagined not having anyone to follow, getting lost and ending up in the wrong classroom while everyone looked at me funny. Then finally making it to the class I was supposed to be in, but late. The teacher would then get mad at me, and everyone would stop and stare. I wouldn't be able to make friends since students went different ways to different classes. I scared myself with so many over the top scenarios I created. I blew things out of proportion in my head a lot.

Not long after that tour, two camp counselors came in to talk about the infamous sixth grade trip we would go on the following year. That was a big deal because we would be staying a couple nights away from home. The camp was supposed to educate us by simulating the Underground Railroad.

I was terrified of this trip. My circling scenario was this image of a counselor yelling at me because I lost my team's chance at having beds and shelter for the night when I wasn't good enough at army crawling in the mud amidst pouring rain. Being anxious about it was normal, but I don't think anyone else took it to the level I did.

Overthinking has always been an issue for me, even at a young age. Scenarios and thoughts seemed to swarm in my head anytime I felt the slightest bit of uncertainty or anxiety. It was quite random. I was in my late teens when I got diagnosed with OCD. I didn't really believe or acknowledge it because nothing I was doing looked like OCD to me. I knew it as television portrayed it; A germaphobe, constantly organizing and washing hands. It was portrayed almost like a silly little quirk rather than a diagnosis.

I hadn't realized that what I was experiencing was Obsessive Compulsive Disorder, a life-altering anxiety disorder. Often irrational, these thoughts or scenarios would swarm my head with anxiety, leading me to do something in the moment that could quiet the thought or anxiety. The thing that quiets the anxiety is the compulsion. Sometimes the only compulsion was ruminating on that thought, dissecting it for months. And that didn't rid any anxiety. I even somehow knew the thought was irrational, but at the same time I still couldn't let it go. I obsessed over it and questioned myself in the process. The first big obsessive thought that I can remember was at a baseball game.

Baseball season was a big part of our childhood. Dad would take me and Mark to Minor League games all the time. We never stayed in our seats. Instead, we ran up and down the giant ramps, snuck into different sections, and waited by the dugout for players to throw us a ball. Our favorite was tossing peanuts into the crowd from the very top. While giggling, we would try to play it cool when people looked around confused about the flying peanut.

There were a few times we got to go to a Cincinnati Reds game, dad's favorite Major League team. One time we got there early and decided to walk across the Ohio River next to the stadium. Kentucky was right across the bridge from Cincinnati. I had brought my favorite childhood toy with me in the car. His name was Ducky, a stuffed animal duck if you can believe it. I left him in the car before our walk across the bridge. Instead of the usual reasons someone might not want to bring a stuffed animal to a baseball game, my reason was different.

Ducky went everywhere with me. I wanted to bring him that day. I left him at a restaurant by accident once and cried the whole way home. Dad worked closer, so he called to make sure they had him still. I only stopped crying when I knew the restaurant would keep Ducky safe until dad could pick him up after work.

The day of the Reds game, there was a thought placed in my head. I didn't know who created it or who put it there, maybe it was me. But I over analyzed everything about it. Here was the thought: *If I were to bring Ducky across the bridge, I would have held him over the edge and loosened my grip just enough to possibly drop him.* It was like a trust fall with a 50/50 chance he'd plummet a thousand feet to the river and I'd lose him forever. I don't know why I had that thought, I loved Ducky so much.

The thought of holding him over a bridge even with a tight grip was something I would never want to do, but my mind was telling me I would. The entire Reds game I picked apart that thought and came to the conclusion that I was a bad mother to Ducky for even having the thought. Did I really think I would do something like that? And why? It broke my heart. The scenario went around my head for weeks. I dwelled on the horrific scene of a faded, lonely, yellow speck being taken by dirty water, ending up in the mud somewhere. Breaking my heart over again each time. I had dreams of it even years later.

As a child, these obsessive thoughts happened far and few between, some intense and some not so much. I would spend days or weeks on the intense thoughts, so much that it would always show up in my dreams. They would lead me to question myself and the kind of person I really was. I'd get really upset trying to figure out the meaning of these thoughts without any closure.

The less intense OCD moments were just weird things I mostly grew out of. I could be making toast in the kitchen, hear someone walking from another room, and have to jump up onto the counter. My feet could not be touching the tile if someone was stepping from the carpet to the tile I was on. After their first step, I could go back to standing on it. Id drop everything to jump up onto the furniture in order to make sure someone else took their first step onto the same type of floor as me. I've grown out of that one, but it was the least of my compulsions.

The older I got, the less silly and more anxiety provoking an unfamiliar thought would be. They were harder to muffle, like the scenarios of sixth grade and camp. I specifically remember coming home from school in fifth grade and asking my parents if I could go to a different school the next year.

At first, switching wasn't an option. After more thought, my parents were more open to the idea because this other middle school option would eventually lead me to the high school my mom went to. It was right across the street from my grandparents' home and mom had always loved the idea of her kids attending her alma mater. After much deliberation and *are you sures*, I started my 6th grade year at my new school, part of the church we attended.

We knew a good amount of people who went to that church for school too and they had good things to say. It was much smaller, much less overwhelming, and the classes stayed together all day.

Oddly enough, I liked the idea of uniforms. It was around the time that I started becoming more aware and ashamed of my body. I liked how overly modest the plaid skirts and blouses were, I felt comfortably hidden. I found out very quickly that a uniform didn't change the fact that I was still underneath it. In the lunch line one day, the boys behind me were giggling and all of a sudden, I felt my skirt fly up in the back really quickly. I turned around and they giggled louder. I was the new girl and I was scared to confront anyone so I turned back around and put my back to the wall so they couldn't do it again. I felt my face turn red immediately while I kept them in the corner of my eye. I shook from embarrassment and impatience that the line would move faster. Other than that, I didn't attract much attention at this school.

All because of an Underground Railroad camp, too many hallways, and no one to follow to my classes, anxiety prevented me from following the path originally planned for me. And for nothing. I wasn't a fan of this new school. I never found my niche there. It was extremely hard to make friends, but I had a few. We were the outsiders.

I was on a different wavelength, not mature enough compared to the rest of my classmates. I felt almost like I had covered myself with a cheap paint job to fit in. I was fully aware that they knew it wasn't real, but they were at least nice enough to let me pretend. This was around the time I started realizing that sometimes I felt sad or out of place for no reason. I figured I would grow out of it once I got to high school. Since my parents sacrificed a lot for me to change schools, I stuck it out until 8th grade graduation. Our class fed into two high schools, one of which being mom's alma mater.

3

Becoming Noticeable

Finally, I got to my mom's high school. A much humbler place where many different middle schools fed into. My self-esteem carried over with me at sub-zero. I got along great with all of my classmates; I didn't have bad relationships with anyone. The problem was I didn't truly belong anywhere. I was liked by everybody, I had friends within those walls, but no one close enough to hangout with outside of school. I showed up every day for my first two years of high school trying my best to be worth more to someone.

My sophomore year of high school is when my parents got divorced and my dad moved into an apartment down the road. I wasn't all that surprised about it, nor was it a messy divorce. Later on in a conversation with them, I learned they probably would have gotten divorced sooner but they waited because of our middle school. The normal there was a maintained normal. Not what my family was used to. These families had their cliques, their judgements, and an image to keep up. My parents didn't want us to be the only ones with "problems" who were already not part of the cliques. They waited until we got to high school. This school held all walks of life, all backgrounds. It was normal there to have divorced parents. There was no image to maintain. An accepted normal.

My feelings about their divorce were conflicted. I was sad, but relieved at the same time. I knew they weren't in love. I remember seeing them in the same room, one watching television and the other reading a book, as if they were in separate rooms. I saw them kiss once, it was a small peck before my dad had to go on a work trip. I didn't see them argue too much, but I knew when there was tension.

They were both such great parents to me and Mark. I was less sad for us, and more sad for each of them. I have always been very affected by someone else's feelings or energy. I could feel the sadness in each of my parents as they held themselves together while my brother and I hugged goodbye to stay with the other parent.

I was so conscious of the way I spoke, I never wanted to make either of them jealous or sad. I threw out the word home. Although I grew up in that house, I changed *home* to *Mom's* and I called the apartment *Dad's*. I couldn't label one home and not the other. I had to be fair. I tried not to talk about my time with one parent in front of the other. I wanted them both to be happy so badly. And for a while, I knew they were struggling, keeping it to themselves, trying to hide it. But I caught onto everything and spent too much time overthinking it all.

Maybe I'm not spending enough time with one of them. Maybe they think I have a favorite. Are they lonely without a spouse to live with? Do they cry at night about the situation? What do they do when we're at the others' place? Are they bored? Who do they talk to? Will they ever be happy again?

They were both so strong, but I knew they waited till no one was around to break every once in a while. One evening my dad went missing. We called with no answer. Mark and I rode our bikes to his apartment to check since we had a key. He wasn't there, but his wallet, phone, and car keys were left sitting on the counter. His red car was sitting outside in the parking lot. We could see it from the window of his second-floor apartment.

He had a few things going on right after the divorce. He couldn't stand his new role at work, plus he had to be on call all the time causing him to miss time with us. He had recently been referred to Alcoholics Anonymous after a small incident which put a label on him that we never thought he deserved. He had to attend AA meetings, run errands, and go to work all with a suspended license and someone else to drive him.

My brother and I began to ride our bikes around town looking for him. The police were searching, we called his coworker who said he didn't show up to work and Mom was driving around with my uncle past our bedtime looking. I sat in bed with my forehead up against the window waiting for my mom and uncle to pull up. I listened at the top of the stairs when they got back to see if they had any clues. The police found that the last place he used his debit card was earlier that morning at a certain ATM in our town. I went back to bed and tossed and turned until the phone rang at 6am.

I ran to Mom's room and jumped onto the bed to listen. It was Dad. I don't know what he said, but my mom exhaled, shaking. He was back at his apartment. She made him promise not to move until she got there. My brother and I were to stay put while Mom and the police went over to talk to him and sort out what just happened. He had dropped everything the morning before and just walked. He walked all day with no destination. He said he had walked to a city that wasn't even near us and back. Then he slept on a bench at the baseball fields nearby. He got to a point where he had to shut everything out to clear his head. He was safe. But I knew both my parents were struggling and they dealt with it in different ways. I hated seeing them this way.

I could always feel my mom holding back tears when my brother and I were getting ready to go to dad's apartment. She couldn't always hold them long enough to hide it. It was hard to walk out the door leaving her with just an empty house and her thoughts. It took years to get used to leaving one parent for the other. And it took years for my parents to get used to it as well. But we made it work.

By my Junior year, i was tired of feeling like I had no friends outside of classes. The first day of school that year, I walked up to one of the girls who was always kind to me and asked if I could sit with them at lunch. She immediately got excited and told me she was glad I asked. From that moment on, I was part of something. I had come out of my shell more and more every day. I started hanging out with all different classmates outside of school. I had so many more friends. I was on the tennis team, which became my favorite sport. I was invited to things, I had nicknames, people knew where I lived, boys had crushes on me, I was voted by my classmates onto the homecoming court. The difference between my first two years and my second two years was night and day.

I should have been so happy. I kind of was, but something was still off. There wasn't really a particular reason I felt alone in a room full of people who seemed to like me. Something going on inside my head was putting me down. I had no idea I was depressed and neither did anyone else.

My senior year I was dating a guy I met in a tennis clinic named Spencer. He was a year older than me, we dated for 8 or so months and he was my first love. When he ended it, I took that heartbreak extremely hard. During the actual breakup, I was a dear in headlights, still, and silent. No tears, no eye contact, no rebuttal. Just *oks*. No questions asked. After the moment passed and he hugged me goodbye, I hit a brick wall and everything broke apart. I was crushed.

Just like before, as a high schooler I was still the stereotypical rule follower. I got to class on time, I never cursed, I never got detentions, I was respectful, I didn't misbehave. But less than a week after Spencer broke up with me, I snapped on my Spanish teacher in the middle of class. I argued and raised my voice at her. I then put my head down on the desk so my class mates didn't see the weakness in my eyes filling with angry tears. She was being unfair and I didn't have the capacity to swallow it like I usually did. That teacher was known for being unfair, but never in a million years would anyone guess I'd stick up to her. I could feel everyone's eyes wide, looking at each other in shock, whispers of *Did that just happen?* Silence lingered until the bell rang. I Thanked God for that bell so I could collect myself in between classes.

That incident became the end of my innocent rule following days. I drank here and there with friends before, but on Thanksgiving night, still very heartbroken, I went to a friend's house where I smoked weed for the first time.

I hadn't cursed until I was at one of my classmate's house parties. I was drunk and upset at a guy who messed with my head. We liked each other and he distracted me from Spencer. He knew I had a small crush, but kissed another girl in front of me. Normally I probably would have rolled my eyes and walked away while thinking *eww* if I hadn't still been heartbroken and drunk. Instead I was already unstable and I wasn't with any of my closest friends as I was invited by a different group of friends. It wasn't just a small freak out, I yelled up the staircase at him cursing like crazy, something I had never done to anyone before. I don't think I had ever shown my anger in such an aggressive way in my entire life. Everyone at the party saw it.

That was one of the most embarrassing moments of my life. I remember walking through Senior hallway the next week, everyone looking at me as if waiting for me to acknowledge it. People I barely talked to were giving me high fives. People I didn't feel worthy of speaking with came up to me to ask about it and try to make me feel better. People who weren't even invited to the party had heard about it. Many joked that the guy on the other end of my anger spree was going to get slapped around by his buddies for kissing someone else.

I went from crawling under the radar to being called out by the dean for being dragged across the hallway by my leg although it was funny at the time. I was called out by my teacher because I ran out when one of the boys tried to gross me out. I was reassigned a seat in study hall because Me and those around me wouldn't stop playing around. I was called over by a teacher because I hung halfway out the window grabbing stuff that a friend put outside to mess with me. In the senior superlatives, I was voted "most changed". Although many said it was due to my personality coming out of its shell, I knew there was some other meaning added to that as well. I wasn't sure how to take my new title.

I slowly and accidentally started distancing myself from my friends toward the very end of my senior year. I felt so depressed that I had no motivation to do much if it didn't involve drinking or smoking. I knew it was my fault, but it made me sad that they didn't really seem to care. They moved on so easily without me. After graduation, I had managed to lose contact with almost all of my high school girlfriends.

During that summer, my mom had taken me to a therapist who diagnosed me with Major Depressive Disorder and OCD. This would be the start of trying many different medications for the next 5 years of my life. We all thought the end of my depressive phase was near with help from a professional and medication

That same summer I started working at a country club nearby. On weekends, my coworkers and I met up on campus at Ohio State, where they were sophomores and juniors in college there. We started off at someone's apartment, then hopping around the bars until 2am. The fact that they invited me to everything and enjoyed my company made me feel good. They had already been experienced drinkers and bar-goers, which was still one of the only things I cared to do at the time. I was dealing with my depression by doing these weekend activities. I was numbing myself by drinking, smoking, and being at bars I shouldn't have been allowed into

My high school friends had been replaced by these older college coworkers. My new group was growing as I met more friends through these coworkers as well. At the time, I felt flattered by these guys who wanted me around. In hindsight, it was unsafe. They were older and I had no reason to trust them. They were getting me into bars, making me feel like I mattered, and even voiced crushes. As an 18 year old depressed girl with no self esteem and a broken heart, that was huge. I was desperate to feel wanted by people, I was desperate to feel normal for a night after so much hurt during the week. I put myself in some pretty dangerous situations with people that had no idea what was going on inside me.

Most of the time we all came back to the apartment we started in to crash on the couches and floors. I had fun in the moment, but as soon as I began sobering up in the early morning hours, I was immediately back to broken. The worst part of my week was always the moment I woke up after a night out. I was always the first one to wake up. I'd look around at all the still bodies littering the dark room. I'd tip toe around gathering my shoes. Sometimes I had driven and had to find my car. Other times I'd call an uber or one of my parents to pick me up.

One morning, Dad picked me up from campus after one of those nights out. He knew I was hungover, but not to the extent that I was. I told him I was sorry and I didn't feel well. I had him stop the car in a random parking lot so I could get out and throw up on the ground. He continued to drive me to his house after that. When we got there, I was standing behind him, waiting for him to unlock the front door. I couldn't hold it, I threw up in his flower bed. I figured that would be my lowest moment. I thought life could only go up from there. It was the summer I finally acknowledged that my depression diagnosis may have been right. I thought no longer being in denial would help me get better. I was far from correct.

4

College

The same 2013 summer was my freshman orientation at The University of Cincinnati. Parents were encouraged to go so my mom went with me. I made some friends in my orientation group, but best of all I met my now husband, Noah, in the parking garage afterwards. My mom and I came back to a flat tire on her car. Noah and his dad were walking through when they stopped to help. While Noah changed the tire, we talked and exchanged numbers. We texted that day, and bonded over the fact that we both had Ford Ranger pickup trucks. We became friends, yes, just friends for a couple years.

Noah was dating someone from his high school, so I never really pushed to hang out with him. Coincidentally, some of my friends overlapped with his, so we sometimes ended up at the same parties or events. We would see each other walking on campus and he would throw something at me to get my attention. One year, I lived a few houses down from Noah. We crossed paths a lot.

The first group I joined in college was the co-ed club tennis team. I looked forward to it every week, and I made a lot of friends there. Practice was my favorite part of the week. It helped me a lot to run around and slam the ball. I was good but not great. All I cared about was that I fit in, and I made them laugh. To be honest, it was a huge ego boost because otherwise I wouldn't be fond of myself. I'm not all that funny but being around them made me funny. It was a class clown situation, but underneath I was hiding so much. My teammates made it clear that they wanted me around. I stuck with it for a couple years. I loved the social aspect as much as I loved playing my hardest against amazing players. I surprised myself sometimes.

I loved UC. There were some great memories made there. But my heart was still heavy. I had so much fun when I was around friends doing things. When I was alone, the light switch turned off. I thought college would reset me, It was a new start. I was being prescribed medication after medication, waiting for the perfect combination of mood stabilizer and antidepressant that could make me better. I was dealing with side effects, weaning off one medication and onto another. Nothing seemed to work. I was falling deeper into depression.

One of my medication combinations had me so tired that I would black out completely sober if I didn't go to bed as soon as I took it. Even though I took it at night, I had to leave work early a few times because I couldn't keep my eyes open while standing up. My eyelids were so heavy and my limbs would start to buckle. Ten times worse than feeling sleepy. I was standing up, actively trying to do my job while my limbs felt boneless, like they would collapse if I blinked too long. It took everything in me to lift my eye lids after a blink. It was the worst feeling. Tired was an understatement. No matter how much I slept, the fatigue lasted all day. Basic functioning was not possible.

One time, I was in my dorm room getting ready to go to a bar with friends. As I was getting dressed, my roommates were watching me struggle to stand while putting pants on. I looked in the mirror to take one last look and I don't remember a thing past that. My roommates told me I sat on the floor for a while debating whether to go or not, they convinced me to stay in with them, and I crawled into bed without changing. Apparently, I talked some nonsense for a minute and fell right asleep. I don't remember any of that.

I was driving one morning in Columbus after taking my medicine the night before. I had been home from college that weekend and I started to feel myself falling asleep and becoming lightheaded at the wheel. My grandparents' house was the closest place to me so I drove over there to nap in their bed. I knew I wouldn't make it home. It was scary, I had to stop that medication in order to do life.

I had told my roommates about my depression, and they were supportive. My roommate Cierra was easy to confide in and I even went with her to church once or twice and broke down right in front of her. She was always comforting. A few of my college friends knew I had depression, but it was impossible for me to try and explain. No sickness is easy to open up about. Next to other illnesses, depression wasn't visible. It didn't seem important. There's not a blood test, mammogram, x ray, or MRI/CT scan that could be shown to explain and prove the pain. Depression was a word that got thrown around a lot in conversations. In many of those conversations, depression was reduced to sadness.

Sadness is sitting in a dark tunnel, letting myself feel it. Visitors can come sit with me, but the end of the tunnel is visible and easily accessible. When I am ready to walk out, I can. It's more situational. There is healing. Depression doesn't have an end in sight. It's constant brokenness, that often doesn't come with a reason. It left me helpless and numb. It's more like being stuck in a dark empty room with no visitors, no windows, doors, or way out. Lost hope, lost motivation, lost self. Feeling overwhelming sadness but feeling overwhelming nothingness at the same time.

I wrote most when I was frustrated with my mind. I was never great at writing, but I felt like I needed to. I don't ever remember writing just for myself. I always imagined writing as if someone was over my shoulder trying to understand me. I wrote as if I was answering someone's questions, *what does it feel like? Why?* I liked pretending that the people who never understood mental illness would someday be in an audience while I read everything from my journal behind the microphone. I liked thinking all the people who judge what they don't understand were blinking away blurry eyes in their hidden seats while I unapologetically spilled my heart out in front of them. So much of what I wrote in my journal was to accommodate this imaginary scenario because that's when I picked apart my deepest thoughts.

I wanted to make sense of my pain. I was frustrated and angry that society played it down so much, leaving those of us who truly struggled with a lot more to explain. This is something I wrote part way through college. While writing this, I imagined it as a slam poem, dedicated to all the happy people.

Do you see me? Or do you see my silhouette?
Drawn in colorful markers, reciting memorized lyrics?
Really listen to the song I'm singing.
Do you hear the hurricane in the pit of my stomach?

Where my screams make home of my lungs,
Leaving no room for rationality.
Do you know what that feels like?
It's sitting face to face with the wall that calls me coward
As I bargain for reasons it's worth a broken hand.
But your hands find beauty.
The perfection of the moon pulls your fingertips toward it
But how can something so beautiful be so hardened?
The moon multiplies my loneliness.
I resent it for numbing me until my own hand betrays its dwelling place.
My fingertips do not aim for the moon, but strain for a beauty that can never
be satisfied,
Grazing the dark tunnels that don't tell a soul.
Farther and farther down
In expectation of a peace of mind I'll never get.
My river doesn't drift by with ease.
My river is desperate to desert its miserable territory,
Leaving me thirsty and temporarily paralyzed.

You can use pink bubblegum flavored medicine to rid the bug inside you,
But no remedy can rid the monsters inside me.
For they're more than unwanted company
But permanent monsters that destroy worse things than under my bed.

Embedded in my smile are so many feelings left suppressed.
There are stories that the voice covers with "I'm Fine"
My teeth neglected when I find no motivation to get up and brush them
My lips damaged from being ripped and torn all day by my teeth
My tongue victim of guilt
My eyes blurry, staring right through you
My throat vandalized by knots and nails
My cheeks the compass for lost tears passing through.

Remember that time in middle school you had to read something chosen by
your teacher?
Your eyes move through the words

You're reading through it, but have no idea what you just read
Your mind wasn't in it
That's how I move through life
Going through the motions, zoned out, absent
All emotions shut down and there's no turning back now

Eyes immersed by the floor
It compulsively sends through my most painful thoughts to dwell on
The silence mocks me while scenes wrap around my brain
My mind stuck on repeat
As the rest of the world goes on without a double take
I let it trample me over. I deserve it

You make grocery lists of what you need,
I make lists of reasons I hate myself
Hoping someday those reasons like living on paper rather than in my life
I can't move to get up and fill my cup with water
Or brush my hair, or take out the trash
Only desperation to feel again can uproot me
Don't be naive in thinking this pencil sharpener can only make art
It's an addictive drug offering me sensation of painting red on my body absent
of brush strokes

No one thinks that's beautiful, but why can't it be?
Is it so wrong to long for adrenaline that reminds me I still exist?
Do you know how empty someone must be to reach that point?
If you knew, I bet you wouldn't think it's so fucked up
What's fucked up is that suicide joke you laugh at
Because my mind finds comfort in flirting with the idea of your punchline

Driving becomes a controversy between impulse and heart
Tell me, how can you be windows down, music loud, singing
When you're only a twist away from destruction?
Your fists aren't sore from grasping with concentration
To keep your own arms from betrayal.

The start of an anxiety attack awaits
My heart struggles to escape its prison
My hands rattle to the syllables of each intrusive thought
My stomach feels as if I've skipped a step on the staircase
My stomach always holds my heart

Don't tell me I have no reason to be upset
As if I'm not guilty enough for feeling this way
Don't belittle my illness because you can't see it
Don't turn your head away because you can't hear it
There is nothing more isolating than that

I used to look online for answers. I would search for reasons someone might become depressed, how to explain the feeling. I'd come across so much of the same. *Think positive. It's all in your head. It's a mindset thing. Choose Happiness.* People would compare. *I get sad too, give it time.* It wasn't that easy. I hated letting people think that it was.

5

Trigger Warning: Self Harm

I had a good number of friends, but all from different friend groups. It's hard to explain, but I felt like a floater, never really a core member of a group. I never had that one dedicated group of friends. It may have been all in my head, but I felt like I was the pack of gum at the register someone decided to grab while buying the groceries they came for. I wasn't often on the group's grocery list, but I usually ended up in the cart because someone in the group wanted me. But once the pack of gum was brought back, the group was glad to chew it, I was the fun little bonus.

I compared myself to the people around me whose friends were all in one group, all together. The love for one another was spread equally to each member. Every time something was planned, they knew exactly who was invited. I was the surprise invite because one or two members thought of me. They all added a different piece to the pie that fit perfectly together. I wanted to be a piece of a pie or at least in the group chat.

There was a night I was sitting in bed feeling unable to fake fine. Two of my roommates started a conversation with me that seemed to be something they spoke about beforehand. Of the four roommates, I was the only single one. They told me I wasn't making good choices. They weren't wrong. They backed it up with the fact that I had been dating around a lot and sometimes didn't come back to the dorm until morning. It was never what people thought. Never sex, it was too scary. I wasn't the type to go around like that, in fact, I hadn't ever done that yet with anyone. I just needed human contact, someone to cuddle and keep me from too deep of a sleep. I didn't want to dream, my dreams were always bad. But I didn't want to lay awake alone with my thoughts either.

Honestly, I liked being wanted. I wasn't going to turn down a nice guy if he wanted to take me out or show me he cared. Of course, I was going to enjoy when someone had a crush on me. I went wrong in some situations when I didn't always have feelings for them back. I was embracing the compliment, filling a void and quite frankly, positive attention that kept me distracted for a while.

I started questioning my morals. I never wanted to play games with anyone's head just to make myself feel better. I was very outgoing, I could have a conversation with a rock. I wasn't off putting unless someone gave me a reason to be. I was friendly to everyone I came across and I guess it got me into those situations sometimes. After I was made aware of my jumping around, I went from not fond of myself to hating myself.

Everyone thought I was this happy little ray of sunshine. I was great at masking. I hid so much pain which took a lot out of me. I began experimenting with self-harm, starting on my wrist. There was one day that I was completely alone in our dorm room. I found a pencil sharpener on my roommate's desk with a loose screw. I used my nail to take it out and steal one of the razors in it. I'd get lonely when they weren't around. Sometimes I would think myself into a darker place, grab the razor and a tissue, and stare into space until the pain could ground me.

It wasn't often that all three of my roommates were gone, but I could still think myself into dark places whether they were present or not. I hid the razor in my shower caddy to take with me down the hall. I'd run the water and use my razor blade in there. The water hitting my open cuts stung a lot, but I let it as I watched a watered down, pinker version of my blood drip down the drain. My tears blended in with the water hitting my face, allowing me to erase the fact that I cried at all. In those showers, every part of me slipped through my fingers leaving behind only the razor. It felt like the only option to ground myself.

During tennis practices, on my back hand swing, the bottom of my racket would rub against my wrist while hitting the ball, opening the cuts. It was tricky to play like that. Some weekends, I would go home and my mom caught onto the cuts. She started a routine of asking me to roll up my bracelets or sleeves to check my wrists whenever I visited. I hated that she had to picture what I was doing to myself. I needed to be sneakier about it. Later that year, I moved the cutting to my upper thigh. High enough that shorts would cover.

Whenever I was home, my mom let me sleep with her because I didn't want to be alone at night. My thoughts wandered too much in the silence. She had a TV in there and the presence I needed. I don't think she wanted me to be alone either. The first two years of college in the summers, I lived back at home in Columbus. I was serving at a breakfast restaurant. On the days I didn't work, I remember my mom texting my brother about keeping me company. I don't know how often that happened, but I do know she was afraid to leave me by myself when she was working. She made sure my younger brother was watching out for me. If he went somewhere, he was supposed to encourage me to go along. I was a grown woman sleeping with her mom and being babysat by her younger brother.

All my young adult life I had bad dreams every night. My dreams had always been vivid and memorable, but now they were filled with anxiety, sadness, and helplessness. I always remembered my dreams, even if I had multiple in one night. Many of them involved being hurt or betrayed by someone I loved. Others involved someone I loved being upset with me for something. Either way, I'd end up uncontrollably crying, trying to talk, but unable to. Sometimes I was desperately trying to explain something through my tears, trying my hardest to yell, but it was only ever a whisper. The other person could put me down all they wanted and I had to fall to the ground struggling to get anything out. Desperation was a major theme. These dreams were recurring and sometimes still to this day they come back.

My other recurring dream was driving. For years I dreamt I was driving my dad's car, but never had enough control of the vehicle. The brakes barely worked, I would be putting all of my weight on the brakes, and have to swerve around other cars, go off the road to avoid crashes. I never knew where I was driving to, but I was behind the wheel and frantic. Driving this car in my dreams must have been my subconscious telling me I have lost control of my own life.

Many of my obsessive overthinking and irrational thoughts started from bad dreams. They felt so real that even when I woke up, I was still struggling with the emotions I was struggling with in the dream. It took a lot to get me out of the mindset. Even then, scenarios would stem from these dreams. For example, my dad had never laid a hand on me, nor had he ever treated me poorly, but in some of my dreams he had. I couldn't understand why my sweetheart of a dad would ever be portrayed this way in some of my dreams.

I didn't want to feel negatively toward my dad. I would have obsessive thoughts then questioning myself and my feelings about him. My compulsions were overthinking and proving to myself that I loved my dad very much. In reality, I didn't need to prove that I never had negative thoughts toward my dad. But because of the mental spiral I went down, I was forced to think I did and forced to fix it.

Another OCD pattern I had was scenarios of either of my parents passing away. I have wanted nothing but the best for them, but these thoughts made me wonder if I somehow secretly wanted them to die. I knew I would be crushed if it ever happened, but confused as to why I couldn't turn off these scenarios in my head. I didn't want them there, it made me sad to think of anything happening to them.

I would begin to question everything about my relationship with them. Times I was mean to them, times I hadn't spent enough time with one or the other, times I asked for too much, times I might have favored one over the other. Overthinking these irrational thoughts often kept me stuck inside my own head as if there was a movie theater inside where I was strapped to the chair, forced to watch everything that could possibly mean I was a bad daughter.

I worried about others to the extent that it affected my daily functioning. My day could be ruined because I saw someone sitting alone at a restaurant, wondering what his or her story was. I would assume the worst and become upset for them. The image of an injured or dead animal stained my mind, had me desperate for answers. Why could something so tragic happen to something so innocent? A car crash, an elderly person stuck in a nursing home, people who committed suicide, their families. All of these were things I couldn't let pass.

I was aware that I could not control what happened to other people, but I had a hard time moving on. It was almost like a sixth sense, I would connect myself to this person, ruminating on the things they must be feeling. My heart would hurt for them, taking up days of my thoughts and attention for people I didn't know or animals on the side of the road. I used to be able to say a quick prayer, hope for healing, and move on with my daily activities. Now I couldn't focus on the things I needed to because I was obsessively worrying about these situations. It was even worse when someone I knew was going through something.

Trigger Warning: Eating
Disorder Behaviors

By mid-Junior year, Noah began reaching out to me more and we would meet up. He was no longer dating someone. We would text sometimes and play a game where we asked each other questions, but if we didn't know or didn't want to answer, we would have to do a silly dare. At some point I had to do a dare, but he wouldn't tell me the dare until the next time we were around each other.

I went to his house for a get-together maybe a week later. He sat down next to me and asked if I was ready for my dare. He had me follow him outside away from the crowd. He dared me to kiss him. I was more than happy to follow through. We started spending more and more time together. The more time we spent together, the more we liked each other.

During all this, I felt like I wasn't a total disaster because I looked forward to something; being around Noah. Early on in our relationship though, Noah spent a semester interning at his job, but in the Florida location. The distance was extremely hard and I was insecure. After work I would often smoke weed on my fire escape at night with whoever would accompany me. I wasn't a big fan of the feeling, but it was better than being alone and sober.

That semester, my depression got to the point that small simple tasks provoked tears because I was just too overwhelmed inside to take care of things on the outside. I cried because my license plate needed to be screwed back on my truck. I cried when I was unable to open a jar of pickles. I cried because I didn't want to go to work in the morning.

When Noah came back to Cincinnati, I had managed to phase out self-harm completely. It was replaced by exercise which gave me an even better feeling. Not only was I releasing the same endorphins the self-harm produced, I was seeing results on my physical appearance. Working out felt productive. I wasn't hiding away after class, I was among other students using the campus gym, bettering myself. It started as an innocent way to feel better. I felt more energetic and confident, especially when going out on the weekends in nicer outfits.

It didn't take long before I surpassed the healthy part of working out. I became obsessed with it. I craved the high it gave me and I loved the soreness of my muscles. I started going to the gym every weekday. I'd spend around 2 hours there, working out every single muscle every time, no alternating. I was pushing my body to the max. I got myself a mini notebook that followed me around the gym to each machine I used. I wrote everything I did in that book. All the numbers, reps, sets, laps, distance, weight, times, everything. I never once read back through any of it. I just carried around a physical form of validation that I was working hard in the gym. Evidence to hold. Maybe it motivated me to do more the next time.

Soon, that wasn't enough. I needed to do more. I started restricting food, avoiding certain food and counting calories. I wrote everything I ate throughout the day. I spent a lot of time in front of the mirror looking for changes or things that needed to be changed. I researched all kinds of weight loss strategies, signed up for stupid and expensive diet pill advertisements. At the time, I thought I was doing everything right. I thought this was self-care, climbing out of depression.

The diet pills joined the notebook with me everywhere. I didn't always follow the directions on the bottle, because whether I was eating or not, I would take them. Those pills always made me feel off. It would feel like my brain was glitching. Not so much my thoughts, but the physical feeling inside my head. I can only describe the feeling as if my head was X-Rayed, and on the screen would show my brain flickering lines of colors like a broken TV screen.

I remember learning about eating disorders in health class during high school. It only took 45 minutes to go over the topic. According to the text, eating disorders are all about body image and the control of weight. There were a few paragraphs about what it does to damage the body physically and a stereotypical picture of a girl with absolutely nothing to her but bones. I turned the page for the next part but that was it. Poof. Eating disorders were all figured out in a few paragraphs and a picture. Then we were on to the next subject.

If only when I felt myself going down that rabbit hole, I could turn the page to a different subject. If only an eating disorder was reduced to a few small paragraphs. Little did I know eating disorders would be the magnitude of a giant pile of text books that take years to read. It makes me sad that we learn eating disorders to be just as simple as the question they ask us: *"Why can't you just eat?"*

If just eating was the solution, eating disorders wouldn't exist. It's a complicated web of codependent issues that make an eating disorder into an addiction. Many of us, whether we realize it or not, are addicts to our own drug of choice. Life for me became all about numbing the pain and pleasing the little voice in my head telling me I would never be good enough. My OCD fueled the eating disorder. With every compulsion/disordered behavior I felt a step closer to happiness, but without knowledge that the finish line was moving. And it was moving toward a cliff.

If any part of my routine didn't happen, my day was ruined. If I skipped the gym, I would obsess about how I could make up for it. If I allowed myself to eat more than I had planned, I'd be upset with myself. I had to make up for my failures to follow the rules. My self-worth depended on how good I was at pleasing my eating disorder. I had an actual written list of rules in my journal to follow. The actions that I thought would lead me to *Good Enough*:

1. Don't eat foods I enjoy a lot, buy bland foods- *I wouldn't eat much If it didn't taste that good*
2. Always volunteer to do more physical things at work- *I wanted to burn calories*
3. Only go grocery shopping when it's absolutely needed- *The less food I bought, the less food I had waiting to be consumed*
4. Avoid the isles with tempting treats- *I thought I had to be in and out quick or I would be tempted to buy more food*
5. Do not eat greasy foods
6. Workout at least X times per week. Over at least X amount of time

7. Avoid going out to eat- *I couldn't control what went into restaurant food*
8. If out to eat, order the thing with less calories or plan to purge
9. Eat really slow- *I heard one time that you get full faster if you eat slow and that stuck with me (although it was never true)*
10. Small bites- *a way to make myself eat slower*
11. Chew gum or drink water when I feel hungry- *Another myth I heard was gum and water can suppress hunger*
12. Purge anytime I feel too full- *I carried an old tooth brush in my purse to help with that*
13. Wait out the hunger until it goes away- *If I was hungry for too long, the hunger and stomach growling would stop bothering me*
14. No more than X calories per day
15. Always stay busy or asleep- *An excuse not to eat*
16. If I mess up or do something wrong, don't allow myself to eat- *Punish myself*
17. Drink water, no juice or caloric liquids- *I thought drinking would be a waste of calories*
18. Take two diet pills before eating anything and before working out

To be clear, everything on this list was a total myth that I believed would help me. This was my self-discipline plan. It made me feel more in control of my life. Following these rules kept me at a safe distance from the way I would lay on the floor sobbing, trying to catch my breath. Sometimes I would feel everything so hard that it was unbearable, other times I felt nothing and longed to feel something. I was either drowning or dying of thirst, there was no in-between.

Crying was poking a tiny hole the size of a pencil into my giant, heavy box of sadness, allowing a slow leak until the tiny hole was closed up or clogged. It wasn't satisfying, the box was still just as heavy, it was painful to watch how slowly the sadness dripped out through the tiniest opening. When it stopped, I was still left standing there with this heavy box, no relief, having to walk around with it gracefully as if I wasn't struggling. It took so much energy to carry.

Sobbing was waiting until I was alone to drop my box and kick it until it broke open and everything came pouring out with no consequence to anyone else. Creating a natural disaster in my own room, and there was nothing I could do but lay in it and surrender. The contents of my box of sadness would flood the whole room, reducing me to a leaf getting thrown around in the hurricane.

Sobbing was my body unable to get to a chair or the bed, just sitting in the middle of the floor, almost howling. I didn't even bother to sniff or wipe away tears, I would just let everything fall out of me. I didn't try to quiet myself, hyperventilating while simultaneously yelling out with each breath. Paralyzed. I'd let the tears soak into my hair, my clothes, the floor.

Then my eyes would sting because there were no more tears left. I had used up every bit of them, dehydrated, dry lips, crusty face and hair. But I wasn't done crying. I'd be laying flat on my back, exhaling more cries until my throat hurt. My body would begin to float in the flood and everything would become still. I'd begin to relax my muscles and close my eyes.

When I was ready, I'd collect the pieces of my sadness and put it all back in the box. With a little more strength and a giant headache, I'd tape together my box of sadness and pick it back up to begin walking again.

7

Resisting Treatment

2017 was my fourth year of college. Noah had interned again, but this time in North Carolina for two semesters. Once Again, we were long distance. I had just landed a new Job that I absolutely loved. I was doing what I wanted, working with adults/seniors who had developmental and intellectual disabilities. It was perfect for my psychology degree pathway, and something I became passionate about. The new job was right across the Ohio River in Kentucky.

There were 26 clients in my section including a blind man with schizophrenia, a man with psychosis, and a woman who talked to her chair. There was an older man who dove into a pool when he was 11, bumped his head, and his brain stayed that of an 11-year-old. There was a deaf man with major OCD and intellectual disibility. If he didn't exactly follow his routines, he couldn't do anything else. There were brothers with fetal alcohol syndrome in their 40's and an autistic man who was an amazing artist. He often drew Mice with diapers on.

There was an adorable man who didn't talk and moved slow as molasses, but you couldn't trust him because he'd steal food or prank people. A man with autism who lost something every single morning, got extremely upset, just to find it in his pocket after all. There was a couple who got engaged every single time there was a party or dance as if it was the first time every time. All of them had intellectual disabilities, they were such incredible individuals. They changed my outlook on life and taught me so much with every special relationship. Unfortunately, I had no idea my mental health would affect this new job.

I had been wrapping up my semester in an Art Therapy and Psychology course. I made friends with the girl I sat next to, Rachel. By the end of our semester together, she was the first person to ever tell me I had an eating disorder. She saw the numbers I had written on my hands in pen of calories I'd eaten throughout the day. She saw me come in with a gym bag and my pathetic snack I called dinner. She saw my energy slowly declining throughout the semester. "I know those numbers all too well" she'd say about my hands. She had gone to treatment for anorexia a year prior. She told me I needed to get an assessment at the treatment center. We talked a lot about her experience, and she gave me a lot of tough love. I told her I would go, but I knew I probably wouldn't.

There was a therapist that I saw for free through my college on occasion who also became concerned. I avoided her concern for a while until she told me she legally couldn't be my therapist anymore if I didn't get an assessment from the specialists. I finally agreed to go because I needed a therapist. I thought I could go to the assessment and be sent away with a *"You're fine, just be careful"*. I thought I could go back to my therapist with the good news to continue normal therapy again. I wouldn't let this mess up the job I finally loved. I didn't want to do treatment without Noah around, as he was still in North Carolina for work.

The place I was referred to was called The Eating Recovery Center (ERC). I followed a young woman back to a dimly lit room. It looked like a therapist's office. She started with small talk, while my mind was screaming to get this thing going. The questions she asked started out unsurprising. *Do you count calories? What do you eat on a typical day? What is your average mood on a scale of 1 to 10? Do you ever feel lightheaded or weak?* I expected these questions. Unable to sit back on the couch, I waited for the interrogation to end.

Her questions became harder. Not harder to recall the answers to, but harder to hear myself say out loud, more personal, awkward, and shameful answers. *Self-harm: where, when, how, why? Suicidal thoughts: describe them. Bowel movements: How are they, how often? Purging: How did I do it, how often, what percentage left my body? My menstrual cycle. Describe my recurring negative thoughts about my body. Drinking: how often, how much, what kind, where, with who, blackouts.* The woman seemed desensitized to what she was hearing in my responses, but as for me, it was the first time I was having to describe any of that out loud. As my answers unfolded, I began to think it all didn't sound so *fine* after all. Hearing it out loud was difficult.

She must have thought I knew I had an eating disorder because the questions ended abruptly, and she went right into describing treatment options before I could ask if I was diagnosed. I let her finish and asked if I really needed treatment. That's when she told me I was indeed sick, which I was not quite ready to swallow. Although I was over 18 and could have walked away without looking back, I felt the urgency in her voice and pressure from my family to try it. After cringing at my own answers to her questions, I let her convince me.

ERC recommended a high level of treatment, but I refused to let it affect my job. I negotiated until I brought them down to the Intensive outpatient program (IOP) so that I could go to work full time and go to treatment part time. I convinced the staff that having this job kept me out of the house, from deep depression, and from feeling worthless, which was partly true. I told them I would do IOP or nothing at all. I would not consider the higher level of care. Reluctantly, they let me try IOP, but I had to make improvements. They kept a close eye on me. I worked during the day and drove to treatment after work for a couple months. I was still declining. I couldn't hold up my end of the deal. They had a meeting and bumped me up to the higher level of care (PHP- Partial Hospitalization Program).

I went into work the morning after I got the news with a handwritten letter in my hand. To my surprise, without hesitation, my bosses hugged me and told me they'd be there when I got back. I took a medical leave from my job to attend full time treatment the following day at the PHP level of care. It was 10 hours a day, 7 days a week. I ended up having to do that for 8 weeks. My days consisted of waking up, going to treatment, then going home for bed. Sometimes I would try to do something after treatment on a weekend night, usually drinking with friends at the bars, which often ended up hurting my recovery. I noticed the staff and peers referred to eating disorder as "Ed". Ed was the personification of the illness. It took me a while to catch on to using the lingo, but I did.

8

Treatment

Treatment consisted of all three meals of the day, snacks in between, and a whole lot of therapy. There were many therapy groups lead by different therapists throughout each day. A few times a week, I would be pulled for a session with my individual therapist. Some of the groups consisted of dialectical behavioral therapy, music therapy, art therapy, yoga, a class lead by the dietician about our bodies, writing activities, open process group, and many more. There were small 15 minute breaks in between our groups. I often looked forward to our only 30-minute break of the day so I could take a nap on a couch.

The treatment center was on the fourth floor of a large building. Our area had a waiting room with a front office to sign in and lockers for our things. Past the door with a padlock was a big hallway lined with large group rooms, the nurse's clinic, individual therapy rooms, two bathrooms, and a kitchen with big round tables. There was one group therapy room that was designated for the adult PHP program, another was for the adolescent PHP program. There were other big group rooms that we used throughout the day.

Our main room (the adult PHP room) was on the corner of the building. Two of the walls were almost all window, facing the parking lot, where the sun would shine through. That area of the room was the big olive green comfy chairs and couches. They were arranged in a large circle. The other half of the room had a long table with chairs around it and a counter with cupboards for activities and materials.

The green chair circle was like our homeroom in the little school we called treatment. We started the day there, used it for some groups, and ended the day there. But we all had a specific chair or couch that was unofficially ours. My chair was one of the ones with its back up against the window. I liked that I could feel the sun shining through on my skin. I also liked the fact that I could turn around and look out the window whenever I wanted. On better days I would look outside with my hands and forehead pressed against the glass, I'd sing "I want to be where the people are" from The Little Mermaid, Part of Your World. I was joking about being stuck in treatment. It always got a couple of pity laughs. The better days seemed rare though.

I was always tired and anxious there. It was obvious when I was having a rough day because I would be laying down, curled up in a tiny ball facing the back of the chair. I'd be cuddled under my sweater with my earbuds in. When groups started, therapists encouraged us to be engaged and sometimes the most I could do was listen from my little cocoon, my sweater, a blanket over everything but my eyes.

Some days I put in more effort. I sat up in my chair and listened, talked, and reflected. During some groups, I would listen while drawing in my sketchbook. It kept me safe by grounding me during tough topics. On better days, I would start to open up a little, but never fully.

Every morning upon arrival we took turns going into the nurses clinic so she could check our vitals and weight. On Mondays, we always got blood drawn for more tests. For every meal and snack we were supervised, no sleeves for hiding food, no talk of food or excersize, no throwing away anything until the very end so staff could check it. And absolutely no using the restroom until 30 minutes had passed after eating.

There was also something called Flush Check. I couldn't use the restroom without a therapist standing outside of the door. I couldn't wash my hands or flush the toilet until I opened the door for the therapist to come in and look around. I was on Flush Check for about 5 of the 8 weeks of PHP. My interpretation was that the staff didn't trust those of us who were put on flush check. We had to earn their trust in order to have privacy in the restroom. They had to be confident that we weren't using behaviors in there.

When someone was unable to complete a meal or a snack, they'd be given a certain amount of this drink called Boost. It contained the nutrients and some of the calories missed. It was easier to drink calories than to eat them for me so most of the time I complied when Boost was needed. When someone couldn't finish the food or the Boost, we had to sit in the kitchen with a staff while our peers went back to the room. We would have to fill out a paper explaining why we didn't finish the meal or Boost. It was like a timeout.

I remember one of those times was during a snack. I had been having a really hard time as my fourth year had come to an end. Most of my roommates were graduating and moving out of the house we stayed in. I was going to be in school for a fifth year because I had failed a class and did not have enough credit hours to graduate anyways. That meant I had to move unless I could get at least 5 other girls to live with in the house. Me and Maria were the only two left who would be staying. We found a place to rent for the next school year with two other girls. I was in treatment during the transition between houses, and I had no place to stay between the time I had to be out of one house and moving into the other.

I was couch surfing, Noah was still in North Carolina for his internship, my parents lived 2 hours away and I didn't want to commute to treatment every day from that far. I woke up one morning late because my phone had died while I was asleep. I slept on a deflated air mattress in a friend of a friend's kitchen because I had nowhere to stay. I had gotten to treatment an hour late. They had already had breakfast and were about to go into morning snack. I picked out what I wanted and sat down, updating my friends and the staff on why I was late.

I talked through much of snack time. With 5 minutes left, the therapist at my table nudged me to let me know I had five minutes. I nodded and finished up my couch surfing stories. By then, I had time to look down at my snack and think about what I had to do. It hit me like a ton of bricks. Sobbing and apologizing, I pushed my snack further away from me and looked at the therapist. I shook my head, and to my surprise she padded my back and mouthed "It's ok". She understood that my emotions were all over the place, I wasn't sleeping, I was stressed, alone, and eating just wasn't going to happen.

As my peers got up from the table to clean up, I begged the staff not to make me drink the Boost and just to bring me the paper. I told her she'd be wasting it because I wasn't going to drink it. She brought it out anyway, but brought me the paper to fill out as well.

A long-distance relationship, a new and extra semester of classes, and moving to a new home were all big things happening in my life. Being depressed drained all my energy. It was already hard enough to go check the mail or shower. Anytime my emotions were heightened in any way, my ability to eat dropped. And on top of my normal mental issues, all of the changing circumstances piled right on top.

9

Unwilling

The treatment team knew that a bunch of unmotivated, food deprived, depressed people would go straight home and to bed. In an attempt to keep us from doing that, we had something called Committed Action Plans. At the end of each day we had to state something specific we were going to do that would be a step in the right direction. Often something we had been putting off, avoiding, some kind of self-care, a challenging, or something uncomfortable. As we went around the circle, someone would write down our committed action plans on a giant white board so we could keep each other accountable.

The next morning, the board would be waiting for us. During the morning meeting, we would tell the group how our committed action plan went. Sometimes a few of us didn't follow through so we talked through that. To us, these seemingly little things were a big deal. Some of my action plans were as simple as scheduling a doctor appointment that I put off for years, cleaning my room, making a phone call, going to the store, doing something social, or to finally get my hair cut after more than a year of putting it off. These things were important whether I knew it or not.

The other plan we had to make was once a week in our exposure response prevention group. Each of us were expected to present on something we would do or eat that scared us normally. As opposed to the daily committed action plans, these were more intense. The point was to expose ourselves to the things that triggered us, and to do so during treatment so we had the support to fall back on. Facing those fears would someday lessen the anxiety we experienced around it. Then we would split off to do our exposure plan, come back and talk through it with the group.

An Exposure Response plan could be anything. Sometimes a peer of mine would go down to the store to find new clothes that fit her nourished body. Her goal was to try something on in the dressing room. This was something she knew would trigger her, but she had to overcome the fear. When we all gathered back together, she processed her shame of having to see herself in the mirror, mourning her old body. Some people would try a fear food and record their experience. This was the worst part of my week. I never knew what to do, so most times my exposure response prevention plan was assigned by a therapist.

There was one week I had found out quite a few of my friends were moving down to intensive outpatient (IOP). All the original people I'd begun treatment with were becoming more free and I was staying back in PHP. There were still a lot of us in PHP, but newer people that I wasn't as close with. All I got that week was off of Flush Check. I could use the restroom without being invaded.

On the day I found out about my friends moving down to IOP, they all presented their exposure response plan during group. I couldn't even watch. I stared out the window with tears coming down my cheek. I was mad at them for moving down to IOP. I was mad at staff for not considering me. How was I supposed to come into treatment every day without the original crew to fight beside me?

I was the only one left to present with absolutely nothing prepared. Without standing up, I just threw my arms up and said I had nothing, tears now dripping all over me. I raised my voice ranting. "Everyone is moving down and leaving me behind!" The therapist let the others free of the awkward silence to go off and do their proposed plan, and she sat with me. I don't even remember what I said but she wiped away a couple of her own tears. She felt for me. She knew making me do an exposure response plan at that time would set me up for failure, so we talked through some things I needed to work on in order to move down, then she got my phone for me and I called my mom. She had me sit in the empty group room to calm myself down. Hearing my mom's voice helped a little.

I didn't realize it back then but there were valid reasons that I was staying in PHP for longer. My mood still wasn't stable, they had noticed my self-harm scars were not healing, but reopening. They noticed I still wasn't opening up fully in group, I was still very depressed, and I didn't have a handle on my drinking. Finishing most of my food didn't mean much if the rest of me was falling apart still.

Even though I was eating more and having to drink Boost less, I was still blacking out. It wasn't just an issue of not having enough food to soak it up, it was an issue of alcohol abuse. I was diagnosed at the treatment center, but I kept that one to myself, I didn't want it. I was not going to claim that label.

One morning I woke up for treatment and had a big hangover. I was mad at myself for the amount I drank, I felt sick, and I felt gross. I didn't show up to treatment. A member of the treatment staff called me multiple times leaving a message to see if I was okay. After a while I finally called back saying I was having a rough day, but they convinced me to come in late. I also had a treatment peer message me. He pushed me to come in despite my rough day.

When I showed up, one of the therapists sat me down and asked me what was going on. I buried my head in my knees. He assumed the obvious; I drank too much last night and I hadn't eaten anything yet. After our talk he let me know I would have to drink a giant amount of Boost to make up for my two missed meals and missed snack.

He walked me to the group room where my peers were, so I could join them while drinking my large cup of calories. I made eye contact with the friend who messaged me. He smiled and gave me a thumbs up. I sat in the corner for the rest of the group staring into my cup, avoiding eye contact with the others. Everyone knew I had a rough morning and I didn't feel like making the silent exchange with each person who was wondering what happened. I had on a huge red Cincinnati shirt, with my hair in a messy bun, unbrushed, with what was obviously failure in my cup. I wanted to stay hidden.

On Fridays, one of our groups was Yoga and meditation. A woman from a yoga company would come in and teach the class. She was very good at tailoring it to the needs of our particular conditions, but I was very closed-minded at the time. To me, yoga meant focusing in on my body. It seemed to put a magnifying glass on myself, feeling the bends and folds in my skin, having to concentrate on something I worked hard to ignore for so long.

No matter what room we did yoga in, I always felt big anxiety. We could have any other group in the same room and I'd be fine, but a bunch of us in one room doing yoga made me panic. For one, I don't like feet. There were bare feet everywhere I turned, the sound of feet unsticking to the mats with every movement, having to put my hands on the mat where many feet had been. That in itself was enough to make me want to walk out.

I also had a problem with the door closed during yoga. When group was in session, doors were always closed which didn't bother me. It was different for yoga though. The air felt too still. It felt like everyone's body heat and deep breaths were just stuck, keeping it all in a room that seemed to get smaller as the class went on. Maybe it was a part of my OCD, or maybe a small form of claustrophobia, but I was not okay with breathing in the still hand-me-down air of my peers.

A bunch of feet, some slightly sweaty people, so many deep breaths, silence except for the sound of feet all over the mats was a combination that made me crawl in my skin. I needed moving air, new air that hadn't been breathed in and out by 15 other people already. Due to my heightened senses during yoga, there was a few weeks where I threw mini tantrums, begging staff to let me skip, storming out when I started feeling too overwhelmed.

My temperament was much lower when I was sick. I was irritable all the time. Little things upset me much easier, little things overwhelmed me, and I was just very grumpy all the time. Hangry was a real thing.

On Thursdays for dinner, PHP would walk to a restaurant chosen by the therapists. Our building was in a very populated area with many choices close by. They wouldn't tell us where until it was time to walk, but for good reason. They knew what a group of people with eating disorders were capable of. We would have talked ourselves into panic attacks. We would have looked up the menu online to see the calories contained in each option. We would have been thinking about it all day, ruining everything the experience was supposed to be about. We would be silent during groups leading up to dinner, minds elsewhere.

The purpose of going out to eat during treatment was to add in real scenarios of eating. Normally our portions and meal plans were followed exactly because dieticians made individualized meal plans for each of us. At a restaurant, the portions can't meet each individual meal plan. We had to learn to accept that we are eating something that we could not have control over, not to get overwhelmed when portions are larger. We were not expected to eat the whole meal if it exceeded our meal plan, but we did have to eat at least enough to match our meal plan.

We were not to order salads, we were not to alter our order in a way that would make Ed happier, and our choice had to be approved by a therapist before ordering. Often a few of us would end up crying in the middle of the restaurant or on the way back. Treatment was difficult.

10

Trying for the Wrong Reasons

It took weeks for me to suck it up and do what I had to do to get out of PHP. As hard as it was, I eventually made my therapists happy enough to move down to IOP. I finally decided I was never going to reach the recovery that I had seen and heard about from others. That was an unrealistic expectation. Maybe recovery seemed like such an amazing place but was actually overrated. Maybe the success I reached in eating was actually all recovery was. Underwhelming. I had my hopes too high. Maybe recovery was just pleasing the professionals, becoming physically healthy enough. I thought I was silly for having the idea that recovery could be both mental and physical healing. That seemed impossible.

My goal was to get back to the real world and continue my job. I didn't believe I could ever fully be okay, but it was good enough for me to consider it recovery. After trying harder, opening up more, and doing what I knew was right, the staff moved me down to IOP level of care. I was able to fake fine again and convince the treatment team my mental health was getting better. On paper, I was better. Physically I was back on track, but mentally I was the same or worse.

The outpatient program I was allowed to move down to was Tuesday Thursday and Saturday mornings, as well as Monday Wednesday and Friday evenings. With this schedule, I was back at work three days a week. Everyone was fooled, including myself, that I was in recovery. I was disappointed that recovery didn't feel better than this, but I accepted it. I was still thinking through my eating disorder brain though. I had learned so much in treatment, but none of it was I willing to use. My reason for wanting out of treatment was to get back to working and being normal. I didn't see a life for me without Ed so I was okay with whatever this thing was that I called "recovery".

Since this lower level of care was only supervising one meal and one snack a day, I let my Ed take over during the time I was on my own. My behaviors came back too easily. IOP lasted some weeks before my therapist told me they were putting me back up to PHP level of care. That's when I discharged from treatment on my own terms in a confusing exchange with my therapist where she tried to talk me out of leaving. My mind was already made. I wanted to get back to my job full time. I thought treatment was just taking precautions that I didn't need. So, on my 23rd birthday in 2017, I deemed myself graduated from treatment. Staff wished me well with so much hesitation. If I had been a minor, they would have stopped me from discharging.

I was not at all ready to be on my own again. I was still very depressed, I was not able to concentrate on anything, I was limiting or skipping meals and working out again. I told myself I was able to control those behaviors just enough that it wouldn't be noticeable to friends and family nor would I need any help. I thought I could continue restricting without getting bad enough to be sick again. If I could use behaviors but still keep up with life, maybe it wouldn't be an eating disorder, but something I could keep at arm's length.

When I left treatment on my birthday, it was one of the most lost feelings I had ever felt. I was supposed to be happy, it was my birthday, I graduated treatment, I was free, it was Saturday, there was a football game that night I was going to, and Noah was back in town. Instead of freedom, I felt alone and sad, like I was in some kind of limbo. In between leaving the treatment center and meeting up with friends, I went home and sat on my bedroom floor. I started to cry while doing sit-ups. I left with no professional support outside to keep me going. None of my friends knew how to support me, thinking the beast inside me was just therapized away at treatment. I was manipulated by my Ed, and I manipulated everyone else.

I pulled myself together after my moment on the floor, got dressed and went to my friend's house. I had still been stuck in my head and I drank a lot that afternoon to try to catch up to everyone else. By 5pm, I was completely blacked out and being carried down the street to bed. Within a few hours of being "free" from treatment, I had proved that I was still fully imprisoned by my own mind.

Work was the only thing going well to keep me afloat. I turned off the depression during work hours, but my eating disorder still came to work with me. Ed was the only one I couldn't shove into the closet until I got home. It was the thing that allowed me to shove the rest away for 8 hours a day. It was another full-time job, a 24/7 kind of full-time job. I was always actively trying to numb by pleasing my eating disorder, constantly thinking about it, constantly planning. I thought that's what all the space in my head was supposed to belong to.

11

A Setback with Grandpa

I managed to tread water during my fifth year of college. I told myself because I went through treatment, I had to be fine. Happiness was something for fairy tales. I couldn't expect so much. I had to prove to everyone else I was fine. Even though I really didn't feel like it, I held up well on the outside. I even posted on social media about my experience in treatment and being stronger than ever. I did learn a lot there, and I was better. But only if better meant going from having a seat in the very top of the nose bleeds at a game to moving only a couple rows up. This seat that was supposedly better had a giant pole right in the way. Better to me meant moving forward, but to another crappy spot.

Since everyone thought I was better, I could let my eating disorder thrive in secrecy. Acceptable coping skills didn't work, so I needed my eating disorder to cope. I didn't care about getting better anymore, better didn't feel good. I only cared about escaping.

I still went home to Columbus every once in a while, for a weekend to see family and especially visit my grandparents as they were entering their 90s. I faked fine even to my family who knew me so well. I think my parents were always cautious and watching, but I didn't give them anything to think twice about. I didn't want to waste more of my life getting help that wouldn't fix me. I also wanted to be strong for my grandparents who were already balls of anxiety themselves. They couldn't know under any circumstance that I was slowly falling apart. I couldn't let them worry about me.

My grandpa's health started declining fast that year. He was getting dementia and was not able to walk well at all. That was hard because he was a staple in my life. A strong man I looked up to now needing to be taken care of. He held a special place in my heart. Visiting and talking to him brought me so much comfort and clarity as to how I wanted to carry myself. He was really good at drawing and we bonded over that because I loved to draw from the time I was a little girl.

My grandpa drove him and my grandma to eat out sometimes and run errands. He shouldn't have been driving in his condition at 90 years old, but it was too hard to break his heart. My mom tried telling him not to drive anymore and his response was "If I can't go out. you might as well shoot me." Eventually his driving ended naturally when he fell and broke his neck. The surgery was not safe for anyone his age. We were told to prepare for two very different outcomes.

His dementia prevented him from knowing what exactly was going on while in the hospital. I took a day off work to drive up from Cincinnati to Columbus. I had to see him. My mom and her siblings were also there. Before the surgery, they had him all set up in bed to be wheeled to the surgery room and let each of us go in to speak to him individually. They did that because they really didn't know how this was going to go. We were pretty much saying goodbye just in case. My brother and I were permitted to go together as one. He was on some medication that made him more out of it than he already was.

He told us he loved us and I could tell in that very moment he may not have been clear as to why, but he was completely aware that he was close to death. We could barely understand him, but he was clear in his goodbyes as if he was ready for the outcome we were preparing for. He talked to both my brother and I as we cried next to him. Before I walked out, he looked at me and said something I'll always hold onto. I'll keep that between him and I, but despite being out of it and not always making sense, he was appreciative of our special bond.

My grandma was the last one to go in. She came back without her glasses on. I never ever saw her without glasses. Ever. She must have been crying a lot. She told us he asked her if she saw the angels on the ceiling. We all hung our heads at that. She blamed it on his mind. Was it the dementia or God's angels? I still fully believe it was God's angels watching over him.

We waited for a long time. I laid down, balled up in the hospital chair. A couple hours went by. The doctor came out and let us know they couldn't do the surgery. They had to revive him after just giving him some anesthesia. He was unable to handle the anesthesia and was resuscitated. They had decided the surgery couldn't happen.

We went to his hospital room afterwards. He thought he was on a cruise ship. He kept asking when the captain would let us explore the boat. He would ask if grandma was having fun and when she's coming back to the room. We sent her off with my mom's siblings to eat. I got me and grandpa markers to draw since that was always our favorite thing. He didn't quite understand using markers in his state of mind. He thought he was drawing with me but he was using a marker to trace the shapes on his hospital gown with the lid still on. I remember him trying to explain his nonexistent drawing to me as he traced his gown and it didn't make sense. I looked at my mom with sad eyes and just kept going along with his ideas.

That was the start of my grandpa's steep downhill fall in his health and mind. It was hard to see him like that. He could barely hear or walk and he wasn't usually with it anymore. He still knew who I was and loved seeing me which was good, but he never seemed to know what was going on. He would call my mom in the middle of the night about having a project at the job he had been retired from for decades, convinced he needed to go in. She would have to talk him out of things to ease his anxiety about something that wasn't real. My grandma kept him busy with jigsaw puzzles, which I loved doing with him when I visited.

My grandma was a fun-loving social butterfly. No matter where we were, she was making somebody laugh. She was such a beautiful soul and I hated for her to go through this as well. I watched her stay so strong while we moved them into an assisted living home, sold their car, and put their home of 60 years up for sale. I visited whenever I was home from college, but it still didn't feel like enough.

12

Trigger Warning: Alcoholism and Suicidal Ideation

My weekdays consisted of work and excessive amounts of sleep. I still loved my job working with the special needs population. I was gaining more responsibility but becoming weaker mentally and physically. There were a few instances where I about passed out, causing a scene, being brought to a chair, being handed juice and crackers. I had surpassed my old ways. My eating disorder was getting worse than it had been the first time. I didn't realize I had gotten that far.

My weekends consisted of drinking. I wasn't addicted to alcohol, but I was abusing it. I drank for the wrong reasons, and when I drank, I drank too much. This actually started in mid college. I told myself and everyone concerned that it was a college phase that I would grow out of. Deep down I was scared for myself, but I didn't want to stop drinking.

My alcohol abuse was by far the hardest thing for me to accept or admit to myself. The world's perception of people who struggle with alcohol or drugs is often tainted. I didn't want the reputation that came with the label. The world never seemed to account for all the pain someone must be going through to be using a substance in this way. It's a mental illness that doesn't get much sympathy. It's hard to understand when you haven't gone through it. I turned away in treatment when they told me I met criteria for a moderate alcohol abuse disorder. I left that out of my list of problems.

A big part of why I drank came from my lack of self-worth. I thought I needed alcohol to be a fun person. It helped me loosen up and mask the pain. My depression made me feel like a deflated balloon, my personality felt flat. It was hard for me to hold a conversation when I couldn't get out of my own head. Alcohol gave me that extra boost where I could be enough, because sober, I wasn't enough.

I drank almost, if not, every time I was around friends because I was so insecure. I couldn't be the lame one while everyone else was having a good time. I put so much pressure on myself to make sure I was easy to have around. I wanted Noah to be proud to have me and not have to explain to his friends why I was being boring or moody. I had to turn my mind off somehow, because if not, at best I would be tolerated.

Alcohol only got me so far, it fooled me every time. My anxiety depended on it to the point I never knew when to stop. Noah wasn't completely innocent either, but as for me, this became a permanent pattern on the weekends, blacking out, saying or doing something stupid, putting myself in danger, or needing to be taken care of. I hated having to ask around to piece together my night. It was a waste of memories. What was the use of going out with friends to make memories if I wasn't going to remember them? These weekends were always followed by hangovers, tears, and deeper self-hatred. Sometimes I would be getting sick until 8pm the following night still from the hangover.

The drinking took a big toll on my relationship with Noah, but somehow, we managed. Each weekend started off with high hopes that I would be good enough without going overboard, I'd go overboard, then be upset with myself the next morning. The nights didn't always end in drunk arguments with Noah, but sometimes they did. The feeling of waking up the next morning, knowing Noah and I were mad at each other but not always remembering why had to be one of the worst. By Sunday afternoons, after a good cry on his chest I'd be back to normal, watching football with his roommates.

Another part of the alcohol abuse was my body dysmorphia. It was so bad that whenever I tried to dress nicer to go downtown, I could never accept my reflection. Going from baggier clothing that hid myself during the week to something acceptable for downtown was a big adjustment. I drank while I got ready often to keep myself more laidback when it came to looking in the mirror or picking an outfit.

I absolutely hated getting ready to go out by myself. I hated doing anything alone but getting ready felt lonelier. Something about that was worse than a weeknight alone where I could just sleep. Weeknights alone were normal, but weekends were supposed to be social time. Friday and Saturday nights I had to be awake by myself, triggering myself in the mirror with every insecurity, drinking without anyone, and having anxiety about showing up to wherever I was going. The drinking beforehand gave me more confidence to walk into the places I was meeting people at.

The biggest reason I drank so much was to numb myself. It took me to a whole different mindset. A *screw it* mentality. I liked that because it made me feel invincible. My passive suicidal thoughts didn't scare me when I was drunk. I could be reckless without reservations. I was invincible, yet closer to death at the same time. It made me feel something different. Adrenalin.

I had this obsessive thought or idea about my existence that pushed me to do these things or compulsions. I was stuck in an endless loop of depression, drinking, depression, anxiety, depression, anorexia, depression, OCD, depression. I didn't necessarily want to die, but I didn't want to live either. I could feel the short-term benefit of recklessness, and I could let fate decide to take me or leave me, but I'd be okay with either outcome. I was convinced I deserved for something to happen to me. I had to do reckless things every once in a while, to reassure myself that I was giving fate the opportunity.

I felt that I had to wave the white flag and yell with my arms up *"go ahead, take me!"* It helped quiet the circling thoughts. Because I was reckless, I could justify existing, because otherwise, I didn't feel deserving of sticking around. At least I could come back to the terrible thoughts inside me and say I tried. I gave God the chance to take my life. It just wasn't my time yet.

I would randomly stray from my friends on purpose, get lost, and walk around in the middle of the night in the city of Cincinnati. I would dare myself to do ridiculous things at parties like jumping out a second story window onto a gymnastics mat, giving myself a black eye. One night I was out with some friends, and someone accidently dropped a glass on the ground, shattering it. I knelt down and began using my hands as a broom, letting the glass pieces cut my skin. My friends grabbed my arms to get me to stop. I shook them off to say I got it until they brought over a broom. I pretended I was just drunk and did that without thinking. I was drunk, but I knew exactly what I was doing, I wanted to hurt myself.

I remember being in a bar called Ladder19 late one night, an old fire station transformed. I was drinking heavily with Noah and his roommates. I was having really upsetting thoughts and pictures in my head that my OCD probably produced and I decided I couldn't be in there anymore. I waited until everyone was turned around, slipped my way toward the door, and decided I was going to walk. I didn't know where, but I wanted to be spontaneous. I was quite drunk, and I got lost.

Where we went to school was right in the city. It was well known that no person should walk alone at night. Every week there was an email from UCPD about some kind of mugging, shooting, carjacking, or burglary. Because of the alcohol, the whole night was a blur nor do I remember the sequence of events. But I remembered that night sometimes walking and sometimes running but I don't know why. I remember having my phone in my hand at one point, and next I remember not having it at all.

At some point on my walk/run, a guy came up and stopped to talk. I told him I was lost but going in the right direction. He insisted I go into his apartment and grabbed my arm. I broke from his grip and ran for a couple blocks. I think I was out running and walking for over an hour, maybe two. God knows this was higher power, but somehow, I made my way back to a house I recognized (Noah's house) and slept on the porch until morning. I got my phone from a random guy who said he found it laying on the street.

I had gone to the liquor store the following day and the guy at the counter told me he had seen me running past a few times the night before. He told me it was dangerous, and he came out to help me, but I kept running. We both giggled as I thanked him for looking out for me. I told him I was just intoxicated as he proceeded to bag up the bottle of alcohol I bought for myself.

Many nights throughout college, drunk or sober, I walked alone at night. I took any opportunity to do so and with headphones in. I knew I needed to be scared, but I wasn't. There were also nights I should not have been behind the wheel. Those were nights I convinced myself that I was sober enough, and I truly believed I was. I wasn't used to not blacking out by the end of the night, so when I was fully conscious, I was unaware of my blood alcohol level and how it effected my body. I didn't realize until I would already be midway through the drive that I hadn't been as fine as I thought. I didn't connect to my body in the way that everyone else could. I didn't know when I was hungry just as much as I didn't know how drunk I was.

I didn't care if something happened to me and almost kind of wanted something to. What I didn't think about was the other people on the road who I could have hurt. I truly believe I had a guardian angel sitting in that passenger seat with me each time protecting me and others on the road.

I was selfish, I was reckless, I made terrible decisions. I was also hurting, I felt worthless, I was mentally and emotionally a mess. I have to remind myself that although it's not an excuse for what I did, it still brings me to the conclusion that underneath someone's bad decision is a good person who is in a lot of pain. And I pay for those times with the shame I carry around. I may not ever forgive myself, but I can have some compassion for the Michelle that was behind the wheel those nights. She was going through a lot. I can have compassion for others who make selfish decisions as well. I have no room to judge.

Something tricky about me was that I could be standing, talking, acting like a normal drunk person, yet have no memory of it the next morning. Most people think of "blacked out" as passed out at a bar or sleeping with your shoes on at the bottom of the stairs (which are things I had done as well). Although there were times it was obvious, there were far more times that I was functional. Friends couldn't tell when I had gone too far. I would seem drunk, but no one knew I was on another level.

I had blinders on to the fact that my Anorexia put my tolerance for alcohol at ground level. I'd starve all day, force myself to eat something small before drinking, and that was it. I was so delusional that I thought eating a single slice of bread before drinking was a good try. The cycle was vicious. Eating close to nothing, getting too drunk, getting sick the whole next day, not eating because I'm too sick, repeat. My body was shutting down on itself.

I will never be able to explain the feeling of wanting to drink so badly while knowing I would go too far and simultaneously still thinking I could catch myself before I did. I will never be able to explain how much I hated myself sober, thinking I needed alcohol, but hating myself more the next morning because of the alcohol. I will never be able to explain hating the constant cycle I was in, while simultaneously unwilling to step out of it. I didn't want to give up drinking.

I wrote this in my journal during the time I was going through the cycle of my alcoholism.

I'm sober and I hate myself
"Want to go out?"
Why not.
I've changed outfits 3 times… I need to sip
The mirror is brutal, but I can't move from it
I'm anxious that I won't be fun

I'm tipsy and I don't like myself
"Are you ready yet?"
How can I be if nothing looks good?
By outfit number 6 I settle
It's fine I guess
Just suck in the belly
Take light steps
Keep arms still
I got this

I'm drunk and I'm tolerating myself
Aware that I'm taking up space in this bar
It's harder to suck in with all those drinks in my stomach
I'm laughing and dancing
Wow, I can be fun?
Just one more drink to keep myself feeling good

I'm wasted and I don't give a shit
If I can't see them, they can't see me
If I'm too drunk to care what people think
They're too drunk to judge me
I let loose of all my rules

> *I'm blacked out and I have no thoughts*
> *I'm non existent*
> *I don't remember anything*

> *I'm hungover and I hate myself*
> *How did I get home?*
> *How could I be so out of control?*
> *I messed up yet again*
> *I'm not surprised anymore*
> *Just sad*

> *I fucking hate myself*

My family and Noah knew I was not okay by the end of my fifth year in college. I couldn't hide it well. Even Noah's family knew I wasn't doing very well. I loved visiting them, but they were really good eaters and I had so much anxiety about that. Noah's dad is an amazing cook and everyday they were eating three good sized meals and snacking in between.

For years Noah's family never got to know the real me because I was so dissociated. I was coasting on the need to be liked in order to keep my composure. When I felt it collapsing, I'd get really quiet and excuse myself to recollect. I would often have drinks with them and end up getting very tipsy or too drunk. If they didn't know I had alcohol issues early on, they definitely knew it by this time. I played it off like I didn't get upset at the table, or like it wasn't me leaving remnants of my hangover sickness in their bathroom.

I spent so much of my energy trying to appear put together in front of his family. I was a watered down version that never got to enjoy my time with them. I know they were concerned at times and I hated that my presence was so heavy on them. I was grateful that they met me where I was with so much Grace and still accepted me as family.

13

Navigating Suicidal Ideation

My suicidal thoughts never got to a point that I would have purposefully killed myself. I knew I would never do that. The thoughts were more passive, like "what ifs". It was more of the reckless things I did and not caring if something happened.

It was impossible to navigate the suicidal thoughts when it came to friends and family. How do you work through the guilt and shame of being loved by someone while still feeling suicidal? How do you admit that to a loved one without making them feel like their love isn't enough? What are they supposed to do and say in those moments? How can they not question their importance to you? What about the guilt/blame they put on themselves?

I connected with a song called "Sometimes" by Chelsea Cutler because it was exactly how I felt. My family had so much love for me and I loved them right back, so didn't that mean I should have wanted to stick around? Well, I didn't and that confused me and hurt them. I was a little bit relieved when I heard this song because I thought I was the only one who could be selfish enough to be loved so dearly throughout my life, yet still not care to exist.

It's not that the love I received wasn't enough. It's that I felt undeserving of it. My thought was if I died, it would be sad for my loved ones for a little bit, but in the long run, they could be relieved of all the worrying and inconvenience I put them through. I knew that being around me had to be exhausting for people. Always having to pick me up and deal with my unpredictable emotions and behavior. I used to make lists in my journal of why I hated myself. I had 3 or 4 lists in there. I had absolutely no self-worth, so it was easy to feel undeserving of anything good.

There were spans of time I was crying on the phone with my mom at least once a week with no real reasoning other than, I was just sad. I didn't know why or how to stop, but it was so overwhelming, and I had no one else to talk to about that. My mom cried with me on the phone every time out of concern and a broken heart for me. I imagined her dreading my name pop up on her phone knowing that it was going to be more depressing conversations. I felt like the biggest burden to everyone around me. I wanted to stop taking up so much attention from my brother.

To make matters worse, my loved ones tried but couldn't help. So not only were they not able to help me, but so much of their lives were making sure I was okay. And I hated that for them. I was tired of hurting people around me. And like in the song, there's not usually a root of the pain. It's untraceable. And without having specific reasons, it felt like there was no way to fix myself. I was stuck.

I especially hated that I brought Noah down with me. I was always laying down tired, or staring into space. He wasn't having fun with me anymore. I was always exhausted from trying to pretend I was happy on top of working and doing daily life. It was excruciating to see him sad or mad when I couldn't fake it. I felt undeserving of his love because I knew how miserable he was with me at the time.

I knew he was in love with the Michelle that seemed happy and outgoing, and I wasn't her anymore. I just didn't think at that point that I deserved him at all. I couldn't stop upsetting him. He was so patient with me, and continued to love me endlessly through the hardest times.

One line of the song says "tell me it's over, at least I'm closer". I was waiting for Noah to give up on me. That meant I would have less keeping me here. He would be one less person to hurt if something were to happen to me. At that time I felt like I needed someone to give up on me so I could be closer to giving up on myself. I needed the last straw to break so I could throw it all away.

I can't speak for everyone, but here's what I needed. I didn't know at the time, but looking back, I can see clearly. I wanted someone to just listen. I know it's natural to want to fix. Many will try to give advice, which could in some situations help, but at this point I had already thought about, if not, tried everything. Most of the time, I just wanted to be heard.

I wanted someone to listen without thinking of what they were going to say next.

I needed someone to acknowledge how broken I was, that I was not okay. I wanted validation that what I was going through was really hard. Not that it would be okay in the end. I didn't want to hear the cliche motivational phrases that everything would be okay. Instead, I wanted people to acknowledge that they didn't understand, and acknowledge that I was struggling. No fixing. I wanted safety in that they would never judge me for what they couldn't understand.

I wanted someone to meet me where I was at, mentally and physically. I wanted someone to join me on the floor and sit with me when I'm crying. Many times I didn't want to make the effort to pull myself together, but I didn't want to be alone either. I wanted to have both, someone to let me hurt, but be with me in my sadness. A loving presence, allowing me to move through the emotions. Love needs no words.

Most people in my life, through no fault of their own, didn't know what I needed. Heck, I didn't even know. I did have a friend throughout college who was there for me and did many of these things for me without even knowing that's what I needed. He never pretended to know my issues, he met me where I was. He let me be my unfixed up, no makeup, sad, boring self. He let me sit in my sadness but sat with me as I moved through it. Nate, If you're reading this, I appreciate you, brother. Thank you.

Having depression is lonely. It's a different kind of loneliness. It's heartbreaking to feel out of touch with the rest of humanity. Kind of like you aren't really there, just sitting on the side watching the rest of the world continue on without a second take. I was dissociated. Letting my body go through the motions while my mind was trying not to live it. I think I used dissociation to protect myself.

14

Special Occasions

Holidays always brought on negative feelings when it seemed to do the opposite to everyone else. I never wanted anyone to think I wasn't happy to be around them, but I didn't have an easy way to explain the stress and sadness I felt around the holidays. As a young child, I enjoyed all the holidays to the fullest. As I grew up, the less I looked forward to them, the more I felt heaviness in my heart leading up to them.

In high school and college, my family was still navigating holidays with divorce. Our mom and dad wanted to split their time as evenly as possible, make sure my brother and I were part of the decisions and no matter how hard they tried, it didn't feel right celebrating with one of them missing. It hurt to imagine my dad waking up to an empty house on Christmas morning and it hurt leaving my mom at an empty house half way through Christmas day to set off for dad's. It was the best and the only way it could work, but it just wasn't the same.

Throughout college, my grandparents were getting older and the big family traditions slowly started to fall off as well. They were the glue keeping all the extended family on the same page, but they could no longer accommodate. Every year something else had to change. Every year I saw the holiday cheer become more and more artificial. Maybe it was just me feeling that way because I worried about everyone else.

I was always most worried about my parents on holidays. It felt like the happier the day was supposed to be, the lonelier it was for those who weren't in the ideal family situation or the right mindset. I saw both my parents worry about me and my brother. I worried that they were worried. I watched my mom get left behind by her side of the family because they had their own big family get togethers with their kids having kids. I saw my dad trying so hard to make his new house a home for me and my brother. I felt our family shrink as the families around us got bigger.

I hated the expectations that came with special occasions. I couldn't drop my depression or fill the hole in my heart for a few days out of the year just because it was the thing everyone was expected to do.

Every Christmas, Easter, Birthday, etc.… I tried to embrace the joy that seemed to be the air everyone else was breathing. But it wouldn't transfer to me. Why did negativity and sadness seem to hide around the holidays, allowing more happiness than normal? And why couldn't I jump on that bandwagon? I thought Mental illness was supposed to take a break on holidays. Because everyone else was so much happier on special occasions, I felt even more alone during those times. I had worried about my parents possibly feeling the same way.

On Easter weekend, my mom came to visit me at college and I took her to the small church I had called home in Cincinnati. The easter service was extra bright and cheery during worship. When the pastor began his sermon, the first thing he did was pause so that silence could fill the room. It was powerful because when the music stopped playing, the choir sat down, the lights dimmed, we had time to listen to the silence. To many of us, the silence was louder than the music. It was Easter, but it was also just another day in Cincinnati Ohio. Outside of the church walls, the world was still harsh and hurting.

Then the pastor said something that both my mom and I needed to hear. He took away the expectations of happiness and togetherness to say he knew many of us were hurting even on this blessed day. He took the artificial walls down and acknowledged that it's okay to still be suffering on a special day like today. He said we don't need to pretend everything is fine to fit into the holiday cheer that surrounds us.

His sermon began with a prayer of healing that brought tears to many of us in the room because we could finally take off the disguise. We didn't have to fake fine just because of a holiday or special occasion. My mom and I looked at each other, smiling through teary eyes as he continued on to the easter sermon.

College graduation was another special occasion coming up, so I had to put in a notice at work. Noah and I both decided we wanted to move South after college. It worked out that he could transfer his job to the

Florida location. I was looking forward to a new start as if it would reset my whole mind.

Graduation day was extremely hard for me. My mom drove down from Columbus and my dad and grandmother drove down as well. I should have been so relieved and proud. Instead, I felt like I just barely skimmed my way through college, barely remembering a single thing I had learned my entire five years. I felt like a lousy excuse for a bachelor's degree, a complete phony. Noah and his friends graduated from a five year engineering program and I should have graduated a year before with most of my friends.

I also felt a little bit cheated of my college experience because I had been so depressed through it all. I did have some good memories, but my depression overpowered the good memories. I felt pathetic that I never settled into my own solid group of friends. I felt like something was wrong with me for not fitting into a forever friendship spot like Noah had with all his best friends. No one knew this, but graduation day was a really lonely day for me. I didn't think my parents had any reason to be proud. I didn't really have peers to celebrate with besides Noah and his friends. I felt pathetic for following him around, bringing my family to participate in his plans with his family and friends. I held it together all day while I quietly threw sticks on my fire of self-hate.

Our graduation was spring of 2018. Noah graduated with an engineering degree and a sturdy career right out of college. I graduated with a Psychology degree and no idea who I was or where I was headed in life. All I knew is I wanted to make Florida my new home and outrun the struggles.

I immediately found a therapist in Florida so the storm I left behind couldn't find me here. She was a woman probably in her sixties. She didn't specialize in eating disorders at all. She was a nice lady, but she had no idea how to talk to a 24-year-old about 24 year old issues. During the intake, it came up that I was (as I put it) "in recovery" from an eating disorder and her response was damaging. She told me she never would have known and I must be doing better because I look fine. In other words, as interpreted by me, *You're not skinny enough, You're not sick enough, You're not in control. Restrict Restrict Restrict!*

I saw her two more times after that thinking maybe I didn't give her a fair chance. She asked me about my eating disorder behaviors and she compared it to herself dieting. She lead me to believe that not eating much was totally normal and I could continue my "diet". She even started giving me pointers on small meals with less calories so I wouldn't be guilty for eating. She was basically encouraging disordered behavior. She just confirmed my belief that I was just being dramatic. I was fine and nothing I was going through was a big deal. It was normal.

15

Grandpa's Passing

I needed a job as soon as I moved to Florida so I could pay my part of the rent. I had a couple interviews with companies caring for adults with intellectual and developmental disabilities, and I got offered every one of those jobs. But the hours available were overnight. I knew I wouldn't be able to do that shift. I tried one of the group homes whose shift was a tiny bit better than the rest but I couldn't do it. The company was a mess and I barely got to spend time with the clients during my shift. I was just their maid and chauffeur. I lasted about 2 months.

There was a lot of internal pressure to get a job fast, as well as pressure from others. I struggled with feeling like I had no purpose throughout my young adult life, being unemployed made it much worse. I always had people asking if I had found a job yet. I had people sending me ideas and advice for job searching. All of them were jobs that could never fulfill me, like retail and food service. I compared myself to everyone around me who was already working in their intended careers. I wanted that so badly.

I took a couple weeks to look into jobs that could lead me toward a career. I wasn't familiar with Florida yet, so it was hard to find. It seemed to be taking too long. Every time there was a Now Hiring sign, I would be reminded that I wasn't taking opportunities that were right in front of me. I felt selfish. I was a little resentful because everyone but me thought I should just take any old job for now, until I got a better opportunity. It sounded simpler than it was. It was more complex, much harder being the one who had to take a new job I never wanted with hours I hated.

I gave in and started applying to everything with a now hiring sign. I took the first job that called me back, a restaurant. Being without a purpose in life didn't go away with this job. Food service didn't fill my void.

I didn't get out of bed unless it was for work or to go out drinking. I lost all interest in my favorite things like tennis, piano, artwork, socializing. I was tired all the time, not the kind of tired sleep could ever fix. I realized that I couldn't outrun the darkness I felt in Ohio, not even in The Sunshine State. I took the initiative to try therapy again, but this time someone who specialized in eating disorders along with depression and anxiety, Melissa. She was great and I saw her for maybe 5 months. We worked on a lot and I didn't actually mind therapy with her. As soon as she started recommending treatment to me, I began backing away until I fell off the map. I did not want to go to treatment again. I just wanted to talk through my problems with someone and be done. With that, I went without any professional help for months.

I worked a lot of overtime to avoid reality. Reality was living in some kind of purgatory between wanting to do something more with my life and not wanting to exist at all. Getting better was not an option in my book. I was living with Noah who would eventually realize I wasn't worth anything, invading his world, with his friends, I was just the package deal that dragged him down. Noah had known these friends from interning in Florida before moving here. He had established friends, established memories, and a reason to be in Florida. I had just tagged along. Florida didn't need me. I wasn't doing anything important, good, or close to what I wanted with my degree. I was ashamed of myself. I knew I wasn't good enough for Noah, he was going places and I was stuck on a tiny life raft in the middle of the sea. My only job was staying afloat.

I was a hard worker at the restaurant, and within two months, was promoted to a lead server. The only difference was that I could tell people what to do, which didn't matter because I had no guts to do that. Not only did I lack any assertiveness, I was afraid of confrontation. Anytime I saw confrontation as a possibility, I shrunk myself down to a rug that person could stomp all over. I wasn't getting paid well at all and I was missing a lot of fun things Noah wanted to do with me on weekends.

I was overworked, avoiding my feelings, but there was one thing I couldn't avoid feeling. My grandpa was becoming weaker and getting more sick every week. It killed me not to be near for his final year of life. Whenever I flew in, I made sure to spend time with my grandparents. He still knew who I was. My mom had called me when I got off work one evening to tell me he had become unresponsive but was still alive. She was told it was a matter of a couple days before he would pass. He couldn't talk, open his eyes much, or move his body, but the nurses said he could still hear. I decided to fly home to see him. My mom didn't want me to see him in that condition because it was hard to see. She didn't want my last image of him to be that one. I didn't care, I had to get home. He was my buddy.

My flight to Ohio was about a week later, days after he was expected to have passed. Somehow, he was still hanging on. My mom picked me up from the airport and we went straight to the nursing home. Both my grandma and grandpa lived there. Their little apartment had a small kitchen/common area and a bedroom area. When I first walked in, I hugged my grandma and sat on the couch. The bedroom was right there, no door, it was barely separate from the common area. I avoided looking in that direction because his bed was right there in sight. Even though it was barely separated from the common area, I wasn't ready to walk over and see him. It was sad being in a room without him right there, I never saw my grandma without him. They were joined at the hip. They had the cutest marriage.

I was attempting to have conversation with my mom and grandma, but I don't think I had a clue what any of us were saying. The whole time in my head I was trying to build up the courage to go in there and talk to my grandpa. I started small by just looking over. I could see the shape of him laying there. I had no idea what to say. Would he know it was me? Would I say something cheesy? Was everyone in the living area going to hear everything I say to him? He didn't have his hearing aids in, would I have to yell?

My mom could sense my restlessness to get in there along with my hesitation. She asked if I wanted to go with her and I nodded and followed her over to the bedside. I froze, I couldn't speak, I couldn't touch him. My eyes began to sting. She did the talking for me. "Dad, Michelle is here, she wanted to come see you, this is her hand". I grabbed his hand and held it for a while. He didn't move, but something in his breathing changed. I looked at my mom and she just nodded as if it was expected. A couple minutes went by and I squeezed his hand one more time and headed back over to the couch. As I was wiping away tears, the nurses came in to change his clothes for bed. As they laid him back down, he took his last breath.

They didn't seem to know at first, but then called his name and we all fell silent. No breathing. It was unspoken that he had just passed; less than 5 minutes after I said my pathetic goodbye. I had so much more to say. I missed my chance. He was gone forever. My buddy and mentor. My mom's siblings came back to the nursing home after his passing. They told my mom he waited for me. He held on until I could get there, and that comforted me. I do believe that was not a coincidence. He loved every single one of his grandkids, but him and I had a bond that was different. He and I loved to draw and do art, he understood me and I understood him on a deeper level. I wrote him a letter with everything I didn't get to say and read it aloud at the beginning of his wake.

16

Trigger Warning: The Effects of my eating disorder

The day after the funeral, I flew home and got back to work. The heaviness just kept piling on. I was crumbling. I was trying to hold myself together so my family didn't know how bad I was. I avoided calling, or only called when I was feeling like I could hold a conversation. I stopped taking my antidepressants without talking to a doctor because I didn't think it was helping. I was coasting on nothing. Noah saw it and tried to cheer me up, but he could only do so much.

My energy was depleted. My body didn't have enough energy to give to each and every part of a normally functioning body. Because there wasn't enough to go around, the energy went only to the most important organs. During survival mode, the body is made to prioritize sending the energy to the organs that keep us alive and leave out the less important things. If there were a fire in my home, I would make sure the people and pets got out safely before I ever thought about material items. It would be devastating to lose possessions, but I wouldn't need them. I would risk everything else I own to keep my family and friends.

While survival mode kept me functioning, the less important things lacked. My hair began thinning. My body wasn't regulating temperature well so I was always cold. My legs and arms would fall asleep constantly due to lack of blood circulation. My taste buds weren't really working in that nothing tasted good anymore. My menstrual cycle was messed up. I couldn't sleep, and worst of all, my brain wasn't getting enough nutrients to think clearly.

I had what was called *fog brain*. My short-term memory and focus were digressing and my processing was slow. I wasn't retaining information like I once had, there were gaps in my thinking, I couldn't focus on anything to save my life. My brain couldn't function to it's full potential. I felt like I was living my life zoned out most of the time.

I had also lost most of my hunger cues. I later learned that hunger cues stopped for the same reason an animal can hibernate during winter without food. My body caught on to the fact that it wasn't going to be fed very much. So, when it did get fed, it saved and stored as much as possible of that food and made it so that I could last a long time before feeling hungry. In other words, it slowed my metabolism to stretch the small amounts of nutrients it had left. This is what allowed for my hunger cues to disappear.

Just like an animal hunting for food, its body uses that stored energy when the animal is in need of food so it won't be weak while hunting. That's how I was able to still function. I was so used to feeling run down, I forgot what functioning normally felt like. My body used all of its stored energy to keep me going even when I needed food. This resulted in my stomach organ to shrink. Not the appearance of my stomach, but the actual organ that holds the food. When that organ shrunk, it didn't take much to fill or feel uncomfortably full. Not enough nutrients could be held anymore. Eating a normal portion was uncomfortable and made me feel sick, like it didn't fit. The guilt that came with eating cost way more than hunger. Just like working out gave me a high, the feeling of an empty stomach brought me a similar high.

If you continue this, your organs will shut down and you will die. A threat that never scared me the way it needed to. I would have had to give a shit about myself to be affected by that statement. It was just another item on my list of things I deserved. To suffer.

I started having bad dreams fueled by my eating disorder. I often would be trying to do something normal, but for some reason there was always food or gum in my mouth. No matter how many times I tried to scoop it out of my mouth, it grew back bigger, almost choking me. It was always stuck, hindering my breathing, my talking, my swallowing, and distracted me from what I needed to get done. In the dreams I would always find my way to a trash can and try pulling everything out with my fingers. Whatever food it was would always feel like this giant amount of gum being pulled out in stretchy strings. It would never work. More always grew back. These weren't nightmares, but often caused panic.

My eating disorder had power over me. It was like an abusive spouse I was all too reliant on and too scared to leave. I was addicted to it. I needed Ed behaviors (restricting, fasting, purging, exercise, diet pills, etc.) to feel sane, to be seen or loved by others, to cope. Nothing in my life was going in the direction I needed it to nor could I do anything right. This was the one thing that gave me a sense of control when the rest of my life around me felt like chaos. I thought it was my way to success, because without Ed, I would just fade into the background as my depression took over everything. This journal entry was a list of promises from Ed and I was naive enough to believe all of them.

Nurturance and comfort
A distraction from life's hardships
No more depression
Control over my own life
A way to punish myself because I deserved it
A smaller body, taking up less room
Friends and Noah will love me more
People will think I'm worthy to be friends with
Better self-esteem
An Identity (because I didn't know who I was otherwise)
A way to deal with my problems
Numb my feelings
A project/something to work toward/something to look forward to
Lightweight drinker (much cheaper)
I would be more fun
I would have success in life
Life would be better in general

If I wanted any of those things, I thought I had to prioritize my eating disorder, but doing so came with a cost. My friends and family saw my personality slowly fall out of me. Even my coworkers at the restaurant who barely knew me saw it. I let them watch as I let go of myself, with no pride. It was no secret that I was mentally deteriorating.

17

Trigger Warning: Sexual Assault

I was taken advantage of in different ways while working at the restaurant. I worked harder than many of my coworkers and got stuck doing most of the chores at the end of the night before close. I never spoke up, I just did it. Other than taking on other's work, I had been taken advantage of sexually as well. It started off as just harassment, but slowly got worse.

From the summer before college and all the way to this restaurant job I had experiences of sexual assault. Too many to count. Some incidents worse than others. Some might have been avoided if I had given a shit about myself and some would have happened regardless of push back.

In college, I was naïve. The seemingly little things were just normal college culture in my mind. Most males were fine, but in every crowd, someone had to ruin it for the respectful ones. There were grabs, guilt trips, forced hands. I didn't know it wasn't okay to have to pry someones hands from parts of my body when "no" wasn't enough. I didn't know being pulled out back at a party begging before he let me off his lap wasn't supposed to be normal. When Noah and I were dating, these things happened less because he was with me but it still happened sometimmes.

Aside from some of the lesser offenses in college, at the restaurant was the first time I was aware that what had happened was not okay. For a couple years after, I tried to downplay the memories and thoughts. I was ashamed to talk about it. I didn't want to be forced to think further into it. I just wanted to throw all of it in a box, hand it to God, and let him set it on fire. I wanted it not only to erase from my mind, but to be taken out of my life's timeline completely where it never happened.

Not only once but many times I was a victim of that place. It usually started with a substance. Sometimes I was just handed beer to drink while working, getting anywhere from tipsy to wasted. Sometimes I was offered weed to smoke in the back with some of the cooks. Sometimes I was completely sober. But it didn't matter where I was on the sober scale to those men. They knew I was vulnerable and hurting and they took advantage of that.

I often went to the back office to cry at random times. It was obvious that I was depressed. They all saw my eating disorder unfold, they saw my drinking problem clear as day, and by the time word came out, they all knew I was being sexually assaulted and by whom. They knew I was not okay in the mind or body. And they watched.

It started with a night at the restaurant, where the owner of the store fed me alcohol until I was blacked out. He sat with me, drinking until close. The last I remember was sitting at the table with him. Three workers were closing up and the customers had all gone. I don't have recollection of this exact moment, but he started to take advantage of me out on the patio. I know my coworkers saw it.

I do remember snapping back into consciousness during the middle of it. I was standing with my back to the side of the building, he was holding his body to mine. I could only assume he had been kissing me and copping a feel. He was leaning down so his face was almost touching mine, and his hands on my back under my shirt.

Once I woke up to what was happening, I wanted out of it. I excused myself and went to the restroom to stare at myself blankly in the mirror. I shed a tear or two and got myself together enough to grab a water bottle and walk out to my truck. He was in the parking lot asking me to come with him. He got in his car and I drove home wasted and freshly out of a blackout. I got home to a dark and lonely apartment since Noah was out of town.

I sat on the bed confused and guilty. A friend had asked me to go downtown so I figured going would be the best way to forget about the events earlier that night. I changed my clothes and got a ride downtown just to drink more. That was the first incident of sexual assault, which opened the gate for many more. I thought that was the worst of what could have happened. I was mistaken

One morning, I woke up to a bunch of phone calls from Noah and my family. My head was pounding and I didn't recognize where I was. I looked around and soon gathered enough to tell me I was at the restaurant owner's house. I recognized his dog from the times he came to accompany the owner and saw a picture sitting on the side table of the owner. My clothing was disheveled, and I was sore in one area of my body that could only mean one thing. I had never felt lower than I did right then. I wanted to crawl into a hole and seize to exist anywhere but my own little cave where no one remembered I existed.

The last thing I remember before waking up was the night before, sitting on a rock in the middle of downtown, drunk, by myself, when he walked by and saw me. He told me he'd buy me a drink. I'm sure I looked sad because Noah and I had gotten into a drunken fight while out. Because of the argument, I wanted to leave and he wanted to stay out with friends. So we separated, I finished my drink fast, and I sat on that rock looking at my phone to find a ride home. The rest is fuzzy, I don't even know what I said when he offered a drink nor do I remember getting uo to go get one. But that was the decision that turned everything upside down.

I should have stayed with Noah, or I should have at least gotten an uber quicker. What if I had sat in a different spot, maybe he wouldn't have walked by. I should have said no when he said he'd get me a drink. How could I be so stupid? The next morning this man told me I was blacked out unconscious and he carried me back to his apartment after the drink. As if I was supposed to thank him for that. I was limp in his arms and somehow it was okay to put himself inside of me?

I still think back to the morning I woke up on his couch. I still feel anxiety from the memory of that morning, waking up ina strange place, missed calls from everyone, clothes all twisted and undone, and hurting in the most secret part of my body. That was the worst feeling in the entire world. But I couldn't even cry. I just fixed myself and got home. I felt paralyzed, unable to function, move, eat, cry, or talk.

I got home and couldn't even snap out of the shock. Noah wanted to know everything and I couldn't say it. I didn't want to believe it had happened, and I didn't want to endure all that would come my way if I told him. I hadn't even processed it myself. For a few years I stuck to the story of where I stayed and why, but not what had happened. Numb became part of my personality after this.

There was another guy that worked at the restaurant up front with me. He was always making comments about me. They were compliments that went a little too far. I'd roll my eyes, I didn't think much of it, I knew some guys talked like that. I made sure he knew I wasn't interested and was dating Noah, but then he gave me a card on Valentine's Day, but no one else got one. He handed me the card and told me even though he knew I was with Noah, he had to let me know how he felt.

I shoved it into a box under the counter with my belongings. I didn't pick up the card until days later. He wrote a paragraph inside about how he liked me and thought I was special. I never acknowledged to him that I'd read it. I just kept making sure he knew I was not interested. He was also 39 years old at the time when I was 24. The comments didn't stop and it became more intense.

He started cornering me behind the beer cooler to beg me to kiss him. He was extremely persistent as this happened quite a few times but I never gave in. There were a couple times where he stood behind me when I was taking orders at the front counter, playing it off to the customers like he was helping me. But below the eye sight of customers on the other side of the counter, he would grab my waist and hold it when I was in the middle of taking the order. Sometimes I could take my elbow and kind of push him to stop, other times someone would walk out of the kitchen, and he'd pretend he wasn't just doing that. I'd get done with an order, turn around with wide eyes to tell him to stop. He didn't take it seriously.

I told one of the managers to watch what this guy did when no one was looking. Sure enough he saw some things. That manager asked me if I wanted him to confront the guy, but I just asked him to stick around up front more often instead. It helped give the guy less opportunity to get too close to me. I was more willing to avoid his grabs than let someone confront him. The drama and stress of working next to someone who knew I told on him didn't seem worth it.

A couple of the guys didn't drive. I hated that people took advantage of the fact that I drove. I lacked as much assertiveness as I did the ability to say no when asked for a ride. I gave people there so many rides home. I wondered why they worked somewhere they wouldn't walk to. I wondered how they got to work if they couldn't get home. Would they have had a ride home if I said no?

One of them told me he would give me something for driving him home all week. I got out of my truck and walked to the door to wait for him to grab whatever it was, expecting a few bucks for gas. His brother was home and he introduced me. This doesn't even sound real but right in front of his brother, he picked me up over his shoulder and carried me inside firefighter style. At first, I thought he was totally joking about kidnapping me so I laughed. When he didn't immediately put me back where I was standing and instead put me down on what I assumed was his bed, I became serious.

When I questioned what he was doing, his response was "stay a while". He got on top of me and began trying to kiss me. My *No* was a clear one. I was conscious and sober. It was an obvious no, repeated a few times, but he didn't care. I was turning my head, squishing my cheek into the blanket to avoid the kisses so he went for my neck and stomach. Once most of my upper body was free of his weight, I was able to sit up but not stand, I straightened my arms pushing his shoulders away, but when I did that, he started to unbutton my pants.

I had no words, I just kept shaking my head and saying "nope nope nope" out loud. It wasn't until he stood up to try to slide my shorts off that I was able to stand up off the bed and button them back up. All I could manage to say was *"I didn't want to do that, I have to go."* I wondered what he would have done if I wasn't as persistent to stopping it. The rest of the night I went through the scenario in my head a million times imagining all the things I could have yelled or said to him instead of my pathetic "I have to go." I was so angry at myself for my quiet exit.

Many of these types of things happened to me and it seemed to all flood in after the dam broke that was the first time. Medicating was how I dealt with it. Sometimes I would come home high or drunk from work, barely able to sit up straight, unable to give Noah an explanation. He didn't deserve the stress I put him through. He didn't deserve to be left in the dark, but he also didn't deserve to be hurt by what I could have told him had happened to me.

I still dragged myself into work every time. I made myself show up in all my shame and embarrassment. I had no pride whatsoever, walking in with swollen eyes from crying myself to sleep the night before, shaking from anxiety of having to work alongside the same men who did those things to me and the people who saw and knew, but did nothing. I just let my coworkers watch my life like a soap opera pretending I didn't feel every single one of them waiting for the next scene.

If I had any sort of self-worth, I would have questioned why only one of my coworkers seemed to care about all the things I was going through right in front of everyone's eyes. But being that I thought I was trash, why would anyone else treat me otherwise? I must have had it coming, I probably even deserved it. Obviously, it wasn't that big of a deal since no one else had any sense of urgency for me.

Once parts of those stories got out to more coworkers, instead of seeing that I was broken, some of them took that as a green light. Our phone numbers were posted on the schedule in the kitchen, and a couple of the guys had gotten mine from the wall without my knowledge. A couple of them had texted me for work reasons, but some had ulterior motives. I blocked one guy for texting me a picture I never asked for. I was sexually harassed during work often by what they considered compliments. Every time I walked through the kitchen, eyes scanned. My issues were seen as their opportunity. That made me feel worthless. Like a shell of a person. Nothing inside.

I spent a lot of time trying to block out the trauma. I kept it at a distance. I was convincing myself that I deserved the things that happened. The more I showed up to work despite the situations, the easier I was able to believe it was no big deal. The truth is, even when I was numbing myself with alcohol and anorexia, I still thought about it every single day, I just didn't let myself feel it.

I started refusing to take my breaks even though so much of my self-deprecation stemmed from that place. I was more scared to be with my thoughts and face my feelings than I was to swallow my pride and face the people at work who pitied me or hurt me. It was easier to focus on customers than to focus on me. I was afraid to not be distracted. I was afraid to talk to friends and family about my current state. I was scared to look for another job that I would most likely fail at because deep down, I knew I was spiraling to rock bottom. By ignoring my experiences and avoiding the processing of my thoughts and feelings, I also became a spectator to my soap opera just like everyone else was.

18

The Breaking Point

My brother Mark and cousins, Alyssa and Devan, came to visit me for a week during their spring break. Noah and I got to show them what life was like in Florida. They knew I had some mental health issues going on throughout my life, but they didn't know to what extent. We took them to many of our favorite places. I enjoyed their visit although we were drinking for most of their stay, which was an area of weakness. I somehow managed to hide crippling depression until the last night of their trip.

A few times throughout their stay I had some foggy memories, but I never completely blacked out until the very last night, which scared them. When I came back to consciousness, I was in the middle of sobbing and yelling at them, saying they don't understand me. I can't recall how it started, but I was hysterical and not being very nice. That was when my brother called my mom to say "she needs help. It can't wait." For my brother to say something, I must have looked as unstable as I felt.

The next morning was extremely tense. We sat together in the living room, hungover, and staring into space waiting for someone to speak first. Alyssa was the first to speak. "We're not mad at you Michelle". My eyes filled with tears and all I could manage was a whisper, "Ok". After more silence and staring at the TV, we talked. Everything turned out fine and they weren't angry, just extremely worried. I guess I just didn't take their concern well the night before. On the drive to the airport, I promised them I'd get help and hugged them goodbye, only imagining what they were going to say about me to each other in my absence.

I went back to work for a few days while I was also researching treatment centers. It was a Saturday night at work when I had been standing in the front waiting for the cooks to set an order out for me. One of them began to joke about a time he'd seen me drunk while at work and a few of them brought up things they thought were silly that I did as well. They meant it in light fun, but it stung hard enough to upset me. Of all the stuff that happened in that place, it took a small joke to finally break me. A small joke that made me decide that I didn't deserve for my pain to be everyone's entertainment.

I looked at the one coworker who cared about me, then walked to the back to cry. He followed me in and without having to explain I said I can't do this anymore. He said "I know". I asked him to please start looking for someone to replace me. "This is my two weeks' notice, but if you find someone sooner, I want to leave sooner". He let me leave early that night and reduced my hours at the restaurant until he found someone. With that, I was out of there.

I found a treatment center that treated almost everything psychological. The only thing they didn't specialize in was eating disorders. At this place, I was put in an adult group for depression and mood disorders. Half a day passed before they pulled me out and put me in a new room with different people. I was mad to say the least. They told me I needed to be in the substance abuse group. I was escorted there during a quiet activity, trying to control my sobbing, refusing to participate. When the therapist asked me what was going through my head, I said "I don't think I belong in here". I wanted to focus on my depression, not the substance I was using to make it go away. Of the things I struggled with, depression was the common denominator in all of them. I just wanted to fix that.

There was someone in that group who may have had some other issues like schizophrenia. I never knew if he was going to make sense or go off on a tangent. His mood seemed unstable, and I wondered if he was still doing drugs or just had something else going on as well. Everyone seemed to have some kind of codependent mental illness along with substance abuse. I think I was the only one in that group that was also struggling with an eating disorder. I think most, if not, all of us were battling depression. As the days went on, I was relating to people in this group more and more. Being in the substance abuse group opened my eyes to a more reasonable stance on my substance abuse situation.

I made a friend in group that was addicted to drugs and had been clean for a few months. He had a lot of the same self-damaging thoughts that I did. When we did activities as a group, I often looked forward to his turn sharing because he got me to look inward on myself in a different perspective. Our reasons for abusing substances were similar, but he was accepting of his problem and I was not. I learned more from him than I did the therapist. When the therapist talked, it was their job to fix us and it felt like just that. From a peer with similar issues, I wasn't as closed off to listening.

I spent a couple weeks at this place. I listened, I learned, I accepted, but I could not grow further there. They did not specialize in any eating disorders and did not do individual therapy, it was all group therapy. I needed an individual therapist and more intensive programming. I had originally chosen this treatment center to avoid focusing on my eating disorder, yet I couldn't. They caught me red handed.

This Center had me meet with their dietician. Then they took me to an empty conference room to ask me an endless list of questions. They told me they were going to transfer my information to a treatment center better suited for me.

I went for an assessment at a place in Orlando called Center for Discovery. This place specialized in eating disorders and all codependent mental illnesses/mood disorders. Center for Discovery was a lot like The Eating Recovery Center from 2017. I was admitted immediately and began the partial hospitalization program (PHP). I'll call my time at Center for Discovery, *treatment 2019* and my time spent at ERC in Ohio, *treatment 2017*.

I swore up and down that I wasn't sick enough and needed no help when it came to Ed. I just wanted them to fix my mind and leave the eating disorder alone. Unlike I managed in 2017, I was unable to pull off doing what my treatment team needed me to do this time. I was far deeper in Ed than I ever was before.

I compared a lot. I thought size wise I looked too normal for concern. Normal didn't deserve help, only severe. And my journey to the point of treatment was not dramatic enough to deserve professional attention. I thought people deserving of help had the feeding tube stories, the emergency room stories, near death stories, the caught attempting suicide stories, living in residential treatment before PHP stories. Nothing about my story felt urgent, surprising, or heartbreaking. I was functioning physically, but looking back, I couldn't feel how sick I was because that's all I knew for so long. I was used to coasting on no energy and feeling like shit. That was my baseline. I had forgotten what functioning normally felt like.

Despite what professionals were telling me, the triggering responses from random people were the only ones I took into consideration. For example, at one of Noah's softball games, I was having a conversation with a woman whose daughter had been in recovery from an eating disorder. When I told her I was struggling with that as well, she looked surprised. "Looks like you're doing well now." Those types of comments, although she meant well, made it easy for me to justify that I wasn't sick enough.

Triggers were tricky because they made me feel worse about myself, while I also tried to trigger myself sometimes. Triggering myself helped me to be more disciplined in my eating disorder. For example, there were a couple of movies that triggered me, but I would watch them on repeat. The main character had an eating disorder in one of them. The other one glorified mental illness, making my mental illness look boring. I would read about models and follow triggering accounts on social media. I did things like that to push myself further down.

I was envious of anyone smaller than me, and guilty for taking up a spot in treatment. I was so irrational because not only was I comparing myself to peers, but even to teenagers in the adolescent program. I was an adult entering treatment and comparing myself to kids. My eating disorder was supposed to lead me to success, and if I wasn't the smallest one, I was failing.

Some of my peers in treatment had come straight from residential, the most intense level of treatment. That's where they lived for a specific amount of time, had 24/7 supervision, and doctors onsite. The Partial Hospitalization Program was one step down from that, which is where I started as well as many others did too.

Those of us in PHP who didn't start at residential got triggered by conversation about residential. We didn't want to actually go to residential, we just felt undeserving of help, not sick enough. It wasn't being envious of the experiences in residential treatment, it was being envious of their success at having an eating disorder. That's how success was measured by people with eating disorders.

I learned that it doesn't take a war story to destroy a person. No one should have to prove their brokenness in the first place. I didn't have a jaw dropping story to prove my way in. Many of us didn't. Many of us have been destroyed by a much quieter story than the mainstream. A quiet avalanche that not many could hear, the weight unbearable and just as damaging as the others. There doesn't need to be a climax that has loved ones in tears, a *life flashing before your eyes* type of moment, or a rock bottom that exceeds all others. The text books can't encompass the amount of pain and emotion someone goes through.

Everybody deserves help, even those with stories that seem too "normal" for concern. Comparison to someone else's story could be the difference between getting help or not. It could be the deciding factor between life or death. There is no threshold that defines when you can finally get help. If you're waiting for the right time, you never will. Like myself, there were many more people in treatment who didn't think they were sick enough, but they deserved to be in treatment. They were sick enough. Most of us didn't look like the textbook picture, but all different body types. Size doesn't determine how sick you are. It's the stereotype that keeps so many "normal" people from seeking help and so many "normal" stories from being shared.

19

Treatment- Take 2

Treatment 2019 was harder for me than in 2017. I had gotten past the point where I could keep up with the demands of treatment just to please staff. I came in with no hope and a bad attitude. I was skeptical because I knew how far away I had become from the idea of living happily. I knew from 2017 that I could do what I needed to do, but no matter what, if I didn't want recovery, none of that mattered. I needed to want recovery.

In 2017, I refused to eat but I still could. Food still tasted good, I just didn't let myself indulge. Restricting was harder than eating. But this time I had surpassed choosing. Eating was hard, it grossed me out, I just couldn't do it mentally or physically. By 2019 eating was harder than restricting.

Growing up, we got to eat with our grandparents often. They would come to our house or we would meet them at a restaurant. I always ate what sounded good and I ate when I was hungry. I didn't have thoughts stopping me. Every time, they expressed their amazement of how much I could put away. It didn't bother me, I thought it was funny. Spaghetti with butter and parmesan cheese was my all-time favorite food. I would eat two full helpings, no problem. It was an unwritten rule not to underestimate the amount of spaghetti to cook so Michelle could eat as much as she wanted. By 2019, I couldn't even enjoy my all-time favorite foods.

I was glad I didn't enjoy good food anymore. It was so easy to follow Ed's rules when I didn't have to try to avoid food. I thought I was well on my way to having control over my life, but treatment was going to try and take that control away from me. And they were going to be persistant.

I dreaded small talk. No matter what the conversation was, I always attempted to dodge my current situation. It didn't work considering treatment was the biggest part of my life now. I didn't have much else to talk about. Most people found out I was in treatment within the first five minutes of a conversation. One of the first things people bring up is jobs. *How is work going? What do you do for work? Where do you work?*

I never had a good answer. It seemed so cliché to talk about mental illness. Was it worse to say I just didn't have a job or to say I didn't have a job because I was in treatment full time? Either way, it sounded like I was spoiled for relying on other people while I got my shit together. I was embarrassed and I didn't want anyone to think I was using mental illness as an excuse. How was I going to convince others that I needed to be in treatment if I didn't think so myself? I didn't want to sound like I was looking for pity to justify being unemployed.

Then there were always follow up questions like "how long will you be in there?" and then "have you looked at jobs for when you get out?" They were very valid, realistic questions, but I always took that as someone's impatience or judgment. I assumed everyone wondered why it took so long, why I couldn't be better by now, how I could let Noah take on both of our needs while I was in a treatment center all day. How could I be so selfish to not get better already knowing there were people waiting on me?

I didn't know when I'd get out. And it wasn't soon so I hadn't even begun to look for jobs. I learned the hard way that I needed to take care of myself before I could be useful or begin to care for anyone else. I had to be the focus this time. I avoided myself for years and it got me here. Those on the other side of the conversation didn't know, they weren't in my head, feeling what I felt. I wasn't going to seem sick until they could crawl into my mind and take a look around.

I wasn't honest with Noah about how bad I was doing until I was already in treatment. I felt like I was just sucking everything out of our relationship. I was afraid Noah's family would think I was taking advantage of him. I was afraid they thought lowly of me for taking time off from a job, or not getting better the first time. They never made me feel this way, but if I were them, I would have wondered those things.

I had two options. I could stay in treatment as long as I needed to until I got better, which means I would continue living off of other people with no job. The other option was I could leave treatment early, get a job and feel useful, but mentally I would have continued to bring everyone down, drink myself to blackout, and possibly risk my life by eating disorder or suicide. I was damned if I did, damned if I didn't. Treatment felt like quick sand. If I took my time and went slowly, I could possibly reach recovery. If I rushed to get out I would sink further and possibly never get better.

I was frustrated that I couldn't just get better and I was angry that the staff was attempting to take my Ed from me.

Every day upon arrival, the therapists would get our blind weight and vitals. It became apparent to them that I was moving backwards. During one of my individual sessions with my therapist, Sarah, we called my mom. Sarah explained to her that she had begun looking for open beds in residential treatment centers for me. It was not likely that I would stay in Florida. I would go to wherever they had an open bed.

I didn't want to go and endure 24/7 supervision. I would have to live away from Noah for weeks and I wouldn't have any freedom to let Ed slip through. I was so irrational believing I wasn't sick enough for help, having no idea just how close I was to needing more of it. My eating disorder blinded me. I half accepted that I was sick because of this, but I didn't care. I just didn't want to be depressed. I was stuck because listening to the treatment staff was too hard, but not listening would send me to residential. Quick sand again.

The fact that I had a couple days to get myself together before they would send me away terrified me. Somehow, I barely skimmed the surface, but didn't fall in. The psychiatrist had prescribed me a new antidepressant that I tried for the sake of not moving to residential. Although I cried through each plate of food, had to lay down in the office from feeling sick, I managed to stay at PHP level. That was the best I could do though. I got my vitals out of residential territory but was asked to come into PHP for extended hours. Compared to treatment 2017, this PHP program was weekdays only and starting at noon. Breakfast and morning snack were unsupervised.

My extended PHP hours just added a few hours on Saturday and an hour and a half to my weekdays. On Saturdays there was a meal and a therapist lead activity. On weekdays I had to come in early before the others to have breakfast with Jen and Stacey, the director and assistant director. The rest of the morning was free time. It was highly encouraged to journal or do something productive while waiting for my peers to show up. I usually just grabbed a blanket and curled up on the couches to sleep. There was a dog that roamed around some days of the week and I would cuddle with him as well.

Something in me trusted Jen with some information that I couldn't tell anyone. I pulled her aside to ask her if she could give me any information on STDs. I had gotten my first urinary tract infection ever around the time I was sexually assaulted and I hadn't gone to a doctor. The symptoms online read UTI, but it was too hard to make a phone call, go to a doctor, drive to a place, and pick up medication. I drank home remedies inspired by Google, but it never fully went away. Every time something felt a little off, I thought back to waking up on that man's couch without a clue how I got there. *Did he use protection? What all did he put inside of me? How many people had he been inside before me?*

I ended up telling her part of the story and why I was worried. She let me leave treatment an hour early so I could go to urgent care for a test. She suggested I ask a friend to go with me, but I hadn't told a soul what happened to me so I went alone.

I got to urgent care and rehearsed in my head how I was going to tell the receptionist what I needed. I let a couple people go in front of me, waiting until no one else was around the check in counter. I was almost whispering when she asked what I needed. I asked her for an STD test. I didn't make eye contact, imagining she must have thought I was trash. I held back, but I wanted to explain myself. Tell her it's not what she thinks. I took forever to fill out the paperwork because I was thinking of what to say to her when I returned it. Someone else was at the counter by the time I brought her my papers. I missed my chance. She would forever think I was dirty.

When the nurse took me back, I sat in a chair behind curtains with other patients on either side of them. I could hear every single conversation. I quietly answered the questions they asked while cringing at myself. After questions, I sat alone with restless legs in the curtains for someone else to come in. I wondered how many people the nurse consulted about my vagina before someone came back to my curtain square.

She took me to an exam room with walls and a door to give me time to get undressed. I knew what they were about to do. I saw the crunchy paper, the high up exam chair, the scary arms that come out from the sides I'd put my heels on so they could see every little bit of me. I sat my bare ass down on the paper in a giant paper gown, I was freezing. I had always been anxious at doctors and dentist offices. My least favorite part of the doctor is waiting for them to come in, listening to the footsteps, building up to the intrusive part of the appointment. Were they coming to my room? My feet dangling like a little kid. I was shaking, waiting for the moment they'd come in. I could not have been in more of a vulnerable situation with people I didn't know.

They weren't rude, but they weren't warm people. They didn't acknowledge that I was scared, uncomfortable, embarrassed, worried about the results, and by myself without support. I was just another customer. They searched me with cold tools that hurt. My eyes were tightly closed for every second of it. They sent me on my way with some papers and called me two days later with the good news. It was just a UTI and I was prescribed medication for that. I poked my head in Jen's office and let her know the results as soon as I got the call. She was proud of me for facing that obstacle. She knew I had much more to do though.

She asked me to start attending Alcoholics anonymous meetings at a church nearby once a week. On Monday evenings I drove over right after treatment. I was usually the only girl and the youngest person in the group. Everyone was so kind and shared so much wisdom with me. I never felt unaccepted by all these middle-aged men as they always encouraged me to share. I felt like they were protective of me in a way. It was comforting and obvious that many of them had daughters or young women in their lives that they would die for before someone could hurt her. I had already been hurt, but they wanted to lift me up and show me it would never happen again if they had anything to do with it.

AA was like nothing I had ever been to before. A bunch of dudes being vulnerable, taking turns reading prayers, discussing bible verses, sharing experiences with alcohol, and celebrating these little coins they would get for being sober. I wasn't ready to make a promise of sobriety, it was taken very seriously, and I knew I wasn't going to follow through.

The people in these meetings were very experienced in their sobriety. I felt like it had to be all in or nothing, sober or full-blown alcoholic. I wanted there to be a middle ground. Harm reduction so that I could choose not to drink, but also choose to have a few in social situations that I would control myself. I may have needed complete sobriety at the time, but I wasn't ready. I continued to go and get what I could out of the meetings, I just didn't make any promises to myself or my group. I wanted to learn from them, but not take the actions of sobriety.

20

Values

One morning at breakfast, Jen and Stacey had their laptops for some reason. They not so subtly started the conversation I knew was coming, my lack of motivation. I was fully aware that I was unmotivated to recover. The only thing keeping me there was thinking of my family. I was doing it for my Mom and Dad who desperately needed to know I was in good hands. I was putting them through a lot and didn't want to make it worse by walking out of treatment. I was also there for Noah. He had been so patient with me and I wanted to bring back the parts of me he fell in love with. The conversation didn't get too far because I didn't know where to find motivation within, but I told them I would try. After breakfast, I went back to sleep on the couch.

I knew it was almost time for the others to come in when I would wake up to the sound of therapists walking in to get ready for the day. I would pull the blanket over my face when I started hearing them come in because I knew they were disappointed. Stan was my favorite staff member, one of the therapists, and kind of like the dad of the treatment center. I hated for him to walk by and see me sleeping, I was ashamed, but I didn't feel up for doing anything else.

Many of my peers spoke of their own voice fighting back against the Ed voice. The only voice in my head was a mean one, nobody was fighting for me from the inside. And that's why my own motivation felt nonexistent. Peers talked about how mean their Ed was. I knew what Ed meant, but I wasn't understanding the way my peers could decipher certain thoughts as theirs versus eating disorder's. I also knew that Ed wasn't a literal voice they could hear, but the irrational thoughts they couldn't get rid of, the mental illness inside them.

It scared me that the "voice" in my head was always the same, coming from the same source, and I didn't think they were irrational thoughts. I was so deep and trusting in my Ed that I didn't really hear my own voice at all. I thought the Ed voice was me. I was thinking, talking, and living only out of the Ed brain. There was nothing to decipher. One voice for everything. My own voice had been completely silenced and I didn't even notice.

During a session with Sarah, I explained to her that I didn't like who I was but didn't really know how to change that. She pulled out a huge stack of index cards with a word on each one. They were values. I was to find and lay out all of my values. I sat on the floor with all these cards, but I had a realization while looking through them. I asked "Which ones? The ones I've been living by? Or the one's I wish I would live by?"

Sarah had me briefly talk about which values I had been living by, which got me emotional considering I hated the person I was talking about. This was a person created by a monster. Made up of shallow desires, living values that came from my list of rules and promises of the eating disorder. The Michelle that I wanted to be was silent against Ed and I didn't know how to find her.

Sarah's activity was to lay out the values I want to live my life by. We sat on the floor, I started with any and every card that fell under that umbrella. She then had me narrow down the list. Each time she asked me to narrow down the cards, it got harder and harder to decide what was most important over others. By the end, I had it narrowed down to ten. My next task was to write my top ten values down in my journal and what each one would mean to me. Copied from that page of my journal, here's what I put:

Family/Friends- Support for each other. A sense of belonging. To share true laughter. Personal cheerleaders. Having people who know everything about me, that I can talk to

Inner Peace- God grant me the Serenity to accept the things I cannot change, courage to change the things I can, and Wisdom to know the difference.

Purpose- Contribution to the world. helping others. Having things to look forward to.

Compassion- Kind to all. Empathy. Not judging others. Thankfulness/ Gratefulness.

Mindfulness- Stopping to smell the roses. Being present in the moment. Ability to make memories. Ability to enjoy my time. More spontaneous.

Spirituality/Faith- Clarity. Closer relationship to God. Ability to pray to Him and my loved ones in heaven. Meeting people at church. Comfort from a higher power. Church music to heal my soul. Community

Passion- Doing hobbies that I enjoy. Doing things that fill up my glass. I would feel more in-tune with myself and who I am (Things I am passionate about will be part of who I am). Passion in a career.

Adventure- Trying new things. Gaining experience and knowledge. Spontaneity. Variety in my life. Fun.

Knowledge- To be good at what I do. A sense of accomplishment. Wisdom. Further Education. Learning every day with an open mind. Ability to retain things I learn. Interesting to talk to. Ability to teach others.

Self Esteem- Confidence. Wearing what I want. Eating what I want. People are drawn to a good personality. Assertiveness. Using my voice. Stop letting people walk all over me. Not using alcohol to make others like me.

I explained to Sarah that I felt like a liar to lay out those top ten values. I wanted them to be mine, but I wasn't living them out. I was living out selfish values that I couldn't split from. How could I call these top ten values mine if I hadn't achieved any? She helped me realize that those were in fact my top ten values, and they don't need to be achieved to be important to me. There's no finish line that tells me I can now claim a value. It's something to constantly work at and maintain throughout life.

Even though I had lost my way, I hadn't thrown away my values, I had just put them aside for what made me feel better in the moment. The quick fix. They weren't all of a sudden unimportant to me, I had always valued them. I just needed to physically put my values in front of me and analyze them in order to get back on the path. I decided I would try to begin putting my values first, and try putting Ed's values to the side. I couldn't do it all at once, but gradually.

Because I held onto my only motivation (family) I started to fight for them. I didn't do it for me. As I put in work during treatment for the people in my life, I began to find little pieces of myself. Fighting for my family eventually brought me to an unrecognizable voice later on. It was faint, but compassionate. It was me. I was having small thoughts of my own here and there that didn't line up with Ed. That's when I began standing up ever so slightly against Ed. I could start to decipher the two.

Although I still didn't want recovery, I recognized that I wanted to want it. That was big because it was a step toward motivation from within myself. I had one foot on my own side of the battle field for the first time. I was seeing glimpses of the person I was meant to be. I began to fight for the me I was becoming. I began to see that I could be worth the fight.

When I started to move forward, my safety blankets were all being ripped off. I no longer was permitted to use my old ways of numbing myself. My Ed behaviors protected me from feeling all the things I didn't want to feel. Working on minimizing those behaviors left me vulnerable and extremely fragile, but I had to let myself feel.

I was running through life while covering my eyes. I moved through the basic motions of life without feeling. Treatment's purpose was to pry my eyes open to everything I had neglected. I had to to turn around, look back at all the damage done, and walk back through it. I didn't have to do it alone though. Sarah, Stan, Jen, and all the staff were going to hold my hand and walk through it with me.

Recovering was sitting in the excruciatingly brutal darkness my head created, facing it head on, and fighting it until I began to see light. During that time I questioned whether I would rather go back to my mental illness where it felt familiar and safe or completely break down in a much scarier place called recovery. Healing didn't quite seem like a good thing to me, healing seemed like sacrifice and suffering. But if I was going to do it, treatment was the place.

Recovery from anything always gets worse before it gets better. It's harder to keep going through recovery than to give up and fall back down. But we have to keep our eyes on the reasons we're doing it. That reason sometimes is for other people, and that's okay for now. The further we climb, the more our WHY becomes for ourselves, our lives, our well-being. It becomes something we want just as bad as our loved ones want it for us.

21

Trust

Although I was beginning to open up to learning at treatment, I still took a little while to trust the staff. A little part of me knew they were right, but the biggest part of me still didn't want to budge. Treatment staff got in the way of that. I was very stubborn and had no problem telling staff I didn't trust them. Apparently they were used to it considering people depriving themselves of food can be quite rude.

We each had our own meal plan created by our dietician. They based each meal plan on the specific needs of each person. As time goes on and vitals change, they switch up our meal plans. I was always in my dieticians office asking why I needed X amount of this or that. She never left me without answers. Although her explanations made perfect sense, I still didn't fully believe them.

During meal time, we all prepared our meals together in the kitchen while staff helped and supervised. They held the binders with each individual meal plan in it to make sure we put what we needed on our plate. They caught us if we tried to be sneaky and stiff ourselves on food. They helped us portion out the units of carbs, lipids, protein, and vegetables we needed. It was normal if one or two of us were crying while preparing the meal. The kitchen was a stressful place for us

One day during snack, I was getting my plate ready and chose carrots as part of my snack. I needed about a handful of baby carrots, which was what I got out of the bag. One of the staff told me that since I was at the end of the bag, I should just pour the last few carrots on my plate. I argued a little with her until I slammed the last few carrots down on my plate with tears beginning to gather in my eyes. I huffed and stormed over to drop my plate on the table.

Preparing my meal was triggering enough because of the buildup, knowing I would be consuming it once I sat down, but times like the carrot incident upset me further. They wanted us to get used to realistic situations. She said most people when at the end of the bag, would just finish it, not leaving only 3 carrots for the next person.

Although I didn't know it back then, I needed to be exposed to my triggers in order to lessen their power over me. Action cures fear. On Wednesdays was Exposure Response Prevention. When I first came to treatment, I filled out a fear food hierarchy. Numbering the foods I was most scared or triggered to eat. One of Wednesday's snacks had to be a fear food. When it was time to eat, we each had a piece of paper in front of us at the table. We had to write about how we felt before, during, and after eating it. Our dietitians kept those papers to track any progress. We were encouraged to be detailed. *What kinds of feelings come up, Why do I feel that way, What about this food is so scary, Did anything change from before to after eating it?* There were times I was pissed off and wrote a few words. Other times I had a lot to say.

Those papers for me started off always very angry and vague each week because I was stubborn. I would write things like *I'll throw this at the wall* or *I'm going to blow up* or even as simple as *screw this.* I was convinced that exposure was unnecessary and damaging. Although my papers got more detailed as time went on, I was still having negative thoughts. But at least I was writing them all down in detail. Angry detail still counted as opening up.

I wrote about memories or scenes that would come to mind with that certain food. I specifically had the scene of Matilda in my head where the boy was forced to eat his whole cake in front of the school. I loved Matilda, but I hated that scene. It gave me anxiety. I was eating cookies for my exposure snack one time and after the first cookie, I wrote that I had become that boy in my head.

Another time I wrote about peanut butter being too sticky and thick. I loved peanut butter before I became sick. I ate it all the time. But my eating disorder took away my love for peanut butter. I pictured it getting stuck to the lining of my throat.

One time I wrote on my paper that I was mad at Ryan, a staff member, for making me eat a cupcake with my hands when I tried to use a fork. I hated to get my hands dirty without immediate access to a paper towel, soap, and sink. I know many or most people don't like having dirty hands, but the way I dealt with it was different. I wiped my hands on paper towels in-between every single bite when eating with my hands. I often would wash my hands a couple times part way through, just to come back and keep eating.

Fridays were restaurant days. Staff ordered in food while we all shit our pants overthinking all the unknown ingredients in the food we were about to consume. As an entire category, restaurant food was often a fear food in itself. It was food that I couldn't control or supervise the portions. There's a stigma about eating out versus eating home cooked meals.

The treatment staff ordered pizza and pop one Friday. Because they wanted us to be in realistic situations, they said we could eat pizza on the couches and watch a movie like normal people do sometimes. Some of us had a paper towel and some didn't. Like many foods, I liked pizza up until my eating disorder deemed it a fear food. I got through the first piece, but I was nervous about only getting one paper towel. I watched the movie with my other piece of pizza on the plate in my hand, looking down at it periodically, hoping it maybe disappeared after a while.

I did not want to eat another piece, but one of the staff nudged me and asked me to take some bites to start. I asked if I could get another paper towel before I started eating. No one else had asked for one so they asked me why. I didn't know why, I just needed it. They said I had to try without an extra paper towel because I already had one. But it was used. I would be wiping my pizza fingers with more pizza remains. As I saw it, I was sitting in filth and it made me very uncomfortable and restless.

At this point, my anxiety about a paper towel was more the thing that ruined my ability to eat it rather than the fear of it being pizza. I started bargaining more bites for more paper towel. They said the point is being in a normal situation. Normal people don't get upset about a paper towel, normal people wouldn't be phased by the little bit of dried grease on their hands. I tried to go over to the sink to wash my hands before the second piece of pizza, but they told me no. I would just be getting my hands dirty again.

I sat marinating in anger and pizza grease. I couldn't touch anything. Not my clothes, not my hair or face, not the couch. I just sat there holding my plate above my lap with both hands, building up anxiety about this damn piece of pizza. Staff had called me over to sit with them and eat it. I was already past the point of even trying. I had worked myself up. I began to salt my pizza with tears. It was a whole ordeal. Because of my anxiety, every little thing got me worked up, making it harder for me to eat. My emotions got the best of me that time.

I was called to my dieticians office to discuss the paper towel incident. She asked me about my reasoning and I couldn't give her one. My Ed just hated grease. My emotions were often getting the best of me in situations like these. I may have heard the whisper of my own voice standing up to Ed, but it was still very weak.

22

The Intervention

On an ordinary Thursday afternoon, something in me changed. My therapist pulled me from group for our individual session, then told me that some other therapists wanted to be part of it. That wasn't something that normally happened or that I had ever seen happen in treatment before. Instead of going into her office, she brought me to the table in the common area where a handful of other staff were sitting. I knew an individual therapy session held by 4 therapists and a dietician was not going to be good.

They took turns talking to me about the path I was headed down, the drinking issues, the self-sabotage, the eating disorder, ignoring my prescription medication, and avoiding trauma. They knew I was set on the fact that I was never going to get better. I tried for my family, I got closer, but it was too hard. As I said, I wanted to want recovery. But I couldn't get myself to. I still couldn't want it. They saw me get discouraged and go backwards again.

They asked me about what I dream of for my future. I didn't have an answer for them because I had locked away any sort of hopes or dreams a long time ago. I had dreams for myself when I was younger, but those became darker and darker until they were just gone. Hope was dangerous. Hope felt like setting myself up for disappointment. I also didn't think I deserved a decent future so I didn't allow myself to picture it.

When it came to the treatment team's question, the intervention became clear. Recovery didn't mean anything to me because I had nothing to work towards, nothing to look forward to. I was convinced that I was nothing more than a hollow body taking up space in this world. Getting better meant being thrown back into a world I didn't fit into in the first place.

My treatment team recognized that I held the door to any hope or feelings shut with all of my might. They kicked the door until they got me to peek outside. I saw a part of my mind that I hadn't allowed myself to access. Those dreams weren't realistic to me, but they revealed themselves to me anyways. I told the therapists that I saw Me and Noah sitting on the porch of our home, watching our kids play in the yard before church, chatting with the neighbors in our humble neighborhood. I saw good friends walking in, making themselves at home. I saw career options that I would be passionate about. Last, but not least, I saw a sense of peace in that life. Smiles that hid nothing.

The staff brought me to a place that felt close enough to touch. There was a light at the end somewhere, I just didn't know how to find it. My depression had kept me from seeing any light. Ed kept me from searching for it. All that time, Ed had been in control of me while giving me the illusion of my own control.

No matter how much I learned about mental illness, I always removed myself from the equations. I thought *That won't happen to me.* I had this illusion of control that many of us do. We think we're different than the rest, more careful or invincible.

I knew so many of the effects that mental illness could have on a person, yet I thought those things would never happen to me. I never thought I'd be bad enough to get diagnosed with anything. I learned about alcohol abuse in school, yet I swore I'd never do such a thing. I learned about suicide and I never thought I could ever consider something so terrible. I learned what anorexia would do to my body, but I thought I was in enough control to keep it without the side effects. I read about women who were sexually assaulted and traumatized, but I never considered myself being one of them. I once said "not me" to all of the things that I now sat at this table of therapists to discuss. I was living in the rock bottom I swore I'd never hit, and with my shovel I kept digging.

The shattering of this mindset began with the glimpse of my dreams, and a glimpse of what life would be if I didn't start fighting harder. I became accustomed to rock bottom for so long that I moved in, made myself a home there, but I finally wanted to climb out. How could my illness blind me from the fact that I didn't have to live that way anymore? For the first time ever in my life, I was scared of my eating disorder, my depression, my alcohol abuse, all of it. And I was angry at it for taking years of my life from me.

I could finally see through the glorified image that Ed had presented me. I no longer gave it the benefit of the doubt. The therapists had laid everything out on the table. They showed me a beautiful future next to a future that didn't seem worth living for. I then understood the power of hope. *I couldn't leave where I was if I couldn't see where I could go.*

I decided my eating disorder would no longer define me, instead it would motivate me. All this time I thought my eating disorder was part of me, if not all of me. I hadn't opened my eyes to the fact that I was consumed by something that wanted me dead.

From that day forward, I wanted recovery, and I wanted it bad. And the anger I had at mental illness for taking so much was the flame beneath me. I was ready to actually start trying for myself and my future. I didn't know how, and I was quite afraid, but all I knew is I wanted my life back. The difference between treatment 2017 and 2019 was me.

That Thursday may have been the moment I decided I wanted true recovery, but it wasn't at all a simple step to take. I had to face everything head on if I wanted to physically, mentally and emotionally get better. It was an uphill battle. I wasn't always moving forward, but I kept that door in my mind open so I could remember why I wanted this. I knew choosing recovery was going to hurt a lot, but this time, I was fully on my own team. I was going to give it everything I had.

The morning after my intervention, I walked in with my journal and laid my latest down on the table in front of Sarah to let her read. With tears in her eyes, she hugged me and encouraged me to read it during process group in front of my peers. It read

These four walls hold me hostage
I'm lonely and cold, but I don't try to escape anymore
I unpacked my bags a long time ago
This is my home now.
There's a small hole in the wall
I like it because I can peak out at the world
But I hate it because the faint light coming through makes me vulnerable.
I pace from corner to corner

Writing out everything that hurts me on the walls of the room.
I've made friends with the girl in the mirror
She's always frozen still, a dear in headlights
When her eyes move, they trace the outline of my skin
I feel the judgment, but I can't move away
I close my eyes
So she reads allowed the writing on the walls.
The words wrap around me tight, teasing me for air
I fall down in surrender.
I'm exhausted and brainwashed by this place
For ten years I've been living in this purgatory
The only way out is to fall asleep and never wake up
The girl in the mirror has never allowed me to sleep, but I want to try
The ground is hard and very unforgiving
It's okay though, I deserve that
Once the tears subside I open my eyes
I have never once looked up at the ceiling in here
There's only one thing written up there
It's in different handwriting than the walls
In tiny letters it reads "hope"
I can't remember the last time I had hope
For the first time in my life, I'm scared of this place
For the first time in my life, I'm angry at the girl in the mirror
For the first time in years, I miss the outside world
I want to live my life, but I don't know how anymore.
I punch the mirror, glass falls
All this time there was a door behind it
I came in through that door ten years ago
The girl in the mirror hid it from me
I guess love is blind.
I'm scared, but I open the door and peak out
I don't know how to leave yet
I think I want to, but I don't know
I don't leave yet
But the door stays open, the breeze feels nice
At least I have visitors now

They remind me what the world outside holds for me
They remind me of my once distant dreams of a future
I begin painting over the pain on the walls
Praying for the strength to move out

23

The Real Start

Going through recovery seemed, for quite a while, like going through the stages of a breakup. Ed was the abusive spouse that I depended on too much to leave. Although not abusive relationships, I moved from extremely sad to angry in my past breakups.

In one of my past relationships, I remember the exact moment I went from sadness to anger. I was finally ready to get rid of the things I had of his. I was going to meet up with him to give it all back. Before I went, my mom was helping me by putting it in a box. I stomped out of her room and came back with my perfume. I cracked a smile and said "I'm going to make him miss me" as I doused his things with my scent. And by God, he did. When it came to my eating disorder, my anger helped me move forward. The breakup, like any other, was making space for better things.

There's an Eminem/Rihanna song called Love the Way You Lie Part II. The first one is good too, but I mostly related to the second one. That song was exactly how I felt about my eating disorder at the time. I read the lyrics as if it was about Ed and it was scary close. I used this song to explain my relationship with the eating disorder to Noah, which helped.

I was starting to look for clarity in the moments I was silenced against Ed. *Why can't you just eat?* became the question I was determined to answer. Just because I now wanted recovery didn't mean I could pick up a fork and eat normally again. That's not how it works.

I started writing out a conversation between my thoughts and the Ed thoughts. This was an example of a battle going on in my head as I sat in front of a plate of food. There's no concrete answer to the famous question everyone wants to know. But this was my attempt:

Me: I like pasta, this meal shouldn't be too hard to get down

Ed: You can't eat something you enjoy because you'll eat a lot

Me: I'll just eat some of it. I'll stop before I even get full

Ed: You don't deserve to enjoy food. Don't do it

Me: I can do this. Come on, Michelle. One bite at a time

Ed: Nope, I'm messing with your taste buds and ability to swallow, joke's on you

Me: Okay I won't enjoy it, but I still need to try to eat a little of it

Ed: Remember how much you've already eaten today? Think about that

Me: That's true. It felt like too much

Ed: Yes, This meal would just be adding to you

Me: But my treatment team says I need to be eating this much or more

Ed: They don't know you like I do. Your body kept up with you just fine before

Me: You're right, my body did feel kind of okay when I was restricting

Ed: And you looked better, now you're gaining weight

Me: I'm working on being okay with my body when I gain weight

Ed: You have failed at everything in life, and you want to lose control of the one thing you can have control over? If you can't control what you look like, you've officially failed

Me: I do miss having the control

Ed: If you lose that, you'll never be good enough. You'll be fatter than you already are and no one will like you. You'll never have that circle of friends you long for. You won't be able to have fun because I'll remind you constantly how ugly you are. You will never be happy if you eat this

Me: I want people to like me for who I am, not looks

Ed: but who you are is a bad person who is a burden to others. You deserve to be punished anyway. Let yourself go hungry. Deprive yourself of food.

Me: You're right, I hate myself so much

Ed: And don't forget that high you get from an empty stomach, don't you miss that?

Me: yes, and I hate being full. And I'm not hungry right now

Ed: It's not okay to eat when you're not hungry. That's over eating

Me: So I'll regret eating this if I do, and I'll feel sick

Ed: And you'll just be more depressed because eating will make you feel things that I could numb for you

Me: I don't want to feel, I already can barely be alone, or get out of bed, or have motivation to do any of my favorite things. I'm already too depressed.

Ed: Then keep restricting so you're more numb. You know it works. You can trust this, not your treatment team who wants you to eat.

Me: You're right. I can't eat this

Ed: Good, I'm proud of you. I will protect you

In choosing recovery, I had to eat even when it hurt, even when the Ed thoughts were screaming terrible things. I had to stop drinking. I had to open up, share my trauma to begin working through it. I had to hurt. I knew I was going to be kicking and screaming so I gave recovery permission to kidnap and drag me through the process.

My Ed voice was going to put up a big fight as I went against everything I had been living for. My body dysmorphia was going to shoot through the roof as I experienced refeeding and fullness again.

There was a day I had been sitting on the couch after everyone else in group had gotten up to start preparing their dinner. I froze because I was fixated on how heavy I felt since I had started pushing through more food than I wanted to. I didn't want more calories in my body after following my meal plan for lunch and snack, nor was I hungry. The therapist, Stan, had been sitting with me listening and consoling. He patted my arm to comfort me as I began crying. My body dysmorphia was in full effect. I shrunk away from his hand, grabbed my arm to cover it and said "It's gross". I thought *He's probably grossed out from touching the fat! The poor man deserves an apology for having to put his hand on such a disgusting arm.* I hid under a pillow while trying to catch my breath.

His eyes were wide in concern and disbelief as he gave me the biggest pep talk about my beauty inside and out. Then he explained to me that it was just a feeling about my body, but not the reality. I just wasn't used to feeling so full yet. He talked me down and sent me to the kitchen with encouragement. For much of this stage, I had pushed through tears to eat as close to my meal plan as possible. I wasn't quite there yet, but I was on my way and most importantly, I was trying.

The further along I got, the worse my body dysmorphia was getting. Although body image ideals are only a fraction of what eating disorders entail, there's still plenty to say about it. Almost everyone I met throughout treatment had some body dysmorphia. Looking in the mirror was a painful experience, and sometimes even provoked tears. Not only was I disgusted at what I saw staring back at me, I wasn't seeing myself accurately. I would see everyone else as they are, but the view of myself was severely distorted. My brain was only able to see what I didn't like. And all those things were intensely amplified. I could only see what Ed wanted me to.

Sitting down was really hard for me because up against a chair, my legs appeared monstrous. I hated my upper arm jiggle. I pinched my mid-section, hoping it could disappear. I saw that my cheeks made my face too round when I smiled. Every part of my body made me cringe. Even my fingers, my ankles, and my back.

Body dysmorphia for me wasn't just about how I looked, but how I felt in my own body. Certain ways that I sat or laid down made folds in my skin and I couldn't stand the feeling of it. Honestly, I shifted to uncomfortable positions just to avoid feeling any folds. Treatment told me a million and ten times that folds are normal and healthy but I couldn't believe them. To this day, I still have a bit of trouble trying to allow myself to be comfortable regardless of what my body is doing. This includes sleeping.

I would feel the need to make my steps lighter because I was convinced that if I walked normally, my body was like an elephant stomping all my weight into the ground, as if I would start an earthquake from walking. Running felt even worse. I never sat anywhere without a pillow, blanket, or book to put on my lap. For as long as I can remember, I had always looked for the first thing to cover myself up. It's a habit I still haven't been able to break.

Many people aim to have the hourglass figure body. I didn't care about that. I wanted nothing. No curves. I didn't want to feel anything on my body anywhere. I just wanted nothing on me so I could float through life, taking up no space. I wanted to be able to curl up in the fetal position without my stomach folding over. I wanted my thighs to stay away from each other. I wanted to be able to sit down and my thighs stayed the same size as standing. I wanted to be the girl in my high school textbook on the anorexia page. I wanted to be able to run with absolutely nothing jiggling.

I remember I used to hate shopping. My mom would have to drag me to the store to find clothes when I was young. Her and I would argue because I wanted to wear looser clothes and she wanted me to wear jeans and normal girl clothes. I would have worn a paper bag if she let me. I hated jeans because they showed off the shape of my body. I also remember begging her to buy me boys jeans so they wouldn't fit to my body.

In High school we wore uniforms. Every once in a while we were rewarded with a day where we didn't have to wear our uniforms. But I remember hating dress down days so bad because normal clothes weren't as modest. Sometimes I would pretend I forgot it was dress down day and *accidentally* wear my uniform anyways. Other days I would wear sweatpants and a t-shirt. I didn't want people knowing what I really looked like under there.

Sometimes, I would try to be normal and wear a pair of jeans to school for dress down day. If I wasn't wearing my uniform jumper, I'd think of an excuse to go to the back of the room during morning prayer and the pledge of allegiance. In order for me to feel comfortable standing up in class I had to be behind everyone so I could stand where people couldn't look at me. I hated knowing people were walking behind me in between classes. I wanted my body to be hidden. I don't know what made me that way, but I was like that for a very long time. I may have been the only girl my age to not to own a pair of leggings in high school.

In treatment, I was wearing Noah's shirts all the time. I was hiding in them. It was also easier for me to eat while wearing big clothes because that way I didn't have to feel trapped in them. It made me feel less like I was expanding as I ate. I was safe and comfortable in loose clothes.

As time went on, the staff at treatment started noticing my pattern of baggy clothing. They challenged me to start wearing my own clothes at least once a week. It took me a while to get the guts to wear something that fit. One morning I did it. I had gotten dressed pretty fast, but took about 45 minutes going in and out of the bathroom looking at the imperfections. I fought through it and waited until treatment. I sent my mom a picture of myself. I had on white overalls that were shorts length, and the shirt I had on underneath was an off the shoulder magenta and black shirt. I wore my converse sneakers instead of the old worn out sandals I normally wore. Under the picture to my mom, I said "Wearing my own clothes to treatment today!"

On my way there, my hands were shaking. I was anxious as all hell. My legs were even shaking on the pedals. I brought Noah's sweatshirt to wear over my outfit in case I got too nervous. Walking through the parking lot, I could feel my heart beating in my stomach. I put the sweatshirt on. I didn't take that off until my therapist needed to get my daily blood pressure. I whispered that I had my own clothes on and regretted it. She promised not to draw attention, so I finally took it off and she was so excited. She put the binder in front of her face to keep from drawing attention while she quietly cheered. This was all in the common area so obviously as my peers started coming in, they saw me and made a little scene. It was unavoidable.

Sarah waved over the other therapists to see me. By that time I was red and violently shaking from nerves. I knew it would turn out good, but initially it was scary.

As my body was being restored, my vitals got closer and closer to normal. These numbers, to insurance, meant I was cured. The staff was blindsided as much as I was to find out insurance wanted me to move down to a lower level of treatment. I would now be going to treatment only half the amount of time for the intensive outpatient program. I was moved to this level of treatment only two weeks after the intervention.

I was improving my habits, but mentally I was still in the heart of the worst pain. I had been stripped of my numbing device and expected to maintain recovery habits while my trauma and depression swarmed in. I wasn't ready to take care of myself yet. My recovery was relying fully on this safe space and the support of PHP. Insurance pushed me out and expected me to maintain with only half the support.

I didn't have to ask to know the staff was nowhere near ready to bump me down to less hours. They understood that where I was in the process was the hardest part; actively trying to recover, but fighting every urge to quit. The part where giving up would have been easier than continuing on. No longer numb, having to work through the intensity of my feelings. The hardest part of recovery wasn't having the eating disorder, but healing from the eating disorder. I had only just begun working through the heaviness in my heart.

Because insurance saw some numbers on a piece of paper, I was good to go. This was infuriating. The staff was scared for me and made sure to packed me a giant box of groceries to take home with me because they knew that without accountability, I wasn't going to go grocery shopping or initiate cooking for myself. I knew I wouldn't hold up my responsibilities outside of treatment and so did the staff. We called Noah, my mom, and my dad to let them know I was going to need some extra accountability in order to keep laying the path.

Sarah told me insurance does this to people quite often. It's all about numbers and saving money. It also depends on the quality of each person's insurance as to how long they will pay for certain levels of care. Insurance has no idea that the numbers mean nothing if Ed is still the strongest force inside. I was all too vulnerable in this stage of recovery. Sarah and the others kept me on track while in treatment and Noah got on me a lot more while I was home. I had my ups and downs. I called my favorite treatment friends when I felt like I wanted to use a behavior or had an intrusive Ed thought. They always talked me through and brought me back to rationality.

Luckily by this time I was fully aware of the difference between my rational thoughts versus the Ed thoughts. It was just a tough fight. I started writing a blog in the free time I had gained outside of treatment. I became passionate about sharing my experience with mental illness and recovery. I was finally starting to understand and I wanted everyone else to understand as well.

I often thought I was annoying for talking about mental illness so much. For so long I went misunderstood and downplayed, desperate to make words of it. My mystery was solved, and I wanted to show the world what I found. I didn't want anyone to think I was seeking attention or fishing for sympathy. It wasn't about me, it was about making people aware, but I didn't want to be that person who would get eye rolls.

I questioned myself every time I talked about it. How much was too much? Did people even want to hear about it? Did they want me to shut up already? Did I look like I just wanted attention? I mean everyone goes through hard things, maybe I was just over sharing. I never wanted to seem dramatic.

I remember so clearly a random social media post from an acquaintance I went to school with. He wrote something along the lines of "I hate when people wear their depression on their sleeve for everyone to know. That's when it's about getting attention." I wondered why I couldn't just quietly save myself without having to talk about it.

The world's idea of the word "attention" is usually a negative one. Of course, it can be, but in many situations, it means something much deeper. My therapist and I broke down the idea of attention. It's a basic human need for all of us. It all comes down to wanting to be seen, heard, loved, understood, wanted, and to belong. We've all been guilty of judging others. I had always heard things like "I get sad too", "you'll get through this", "think positive", so this was me bringing attention to my story because I wanted to be better understood, especially by the people who didn't know how hard it really was. Mostly, I just wanted to explain the details of everything, because it was so much more complex than any textbook or website could ever give justice to.

In the same therapy session, I reflected back on the times I was cutting myself in college. When it came to the stigma around "attention", I held a lot of shame for a few of the times I almost wanted someone to see my scars. Was I just hoping for attention? Was I fake depressed if I didn't fully cover them up? I knew why I cut. I was broken and it released endorphins that reminded me I was alive.

The times I didn't try to cover up the marks were a cry for help, in hopes the right person would see and possibly save me. I had been desperate at that time. Those battle scars allowed my depression to be more tangible. I needed someone to see how dangerous my mind was. In a way it was about having the right attention, desperation to be helped.

The same basic human needs were necessary when talking about mental illness. Looking back, I realize how powerful a simple question from someone was. Whether I was willing or reluctant to answer it or not, questions meant the person was trying to understand. It didn't feel like judgment, but like they were slowly adding stones to a bridge that would someday reach my side of the river.

When someone voluntarily wants to hear about it, the shameful feeling of trying not to look eager for attention went away. I didn't want to feel like I was defending the severity of it. I wanted to feel like people cared enough to ask, I wanted it to be informational.

24

Preparation

One afternoon in treatment, we listened to a woman who had beat cancer talk about her experience of leaving the hospital after so long. She was afraid to be hopeful and because of that thought, she hadn't made plans for a future outside of her treatment. Her identity consisted only of her life in the hospital and her sickness. When she wasn't sick anymore, she went back to her home for the first time and she was completely lost, sad and lonely. She started to miss when she was sick.

My first time through treatment in 2017, I hadn't made plans for my life post treatment. Aside from discharging on my own terms and pretending to be happy, I had nothing to look forward to, nothing to work towards, and no interests to fill my time. I had no idea who I was. I had no sense of direction. Just like this woman, I kind of wanted to be sick again because being sick was comfortable and easier than dealing with reality. It's all I knew and who I was.

Treatment is like living in a safety bubble. Because of my lack of hope, I set myself up for failure in 2017. I had no idea how to live without the structure of treatment. I felt like I wasn't going to get anywhere in life. It was an awful feeling. I was still dissociated and non-existent in my own life. I had memories, but they didn't feel like mine. I learned that there is no way I would recover in the same place I had become sick. I had to set up my life outside of treatment to be an environment I would succeed in.

I learned from 2017 that trying during programming wasn't going to be enough. I had to work on recovery outside the treatment center as well. Outside those doors was a cold world, insensitive and unforgiving. I had to prepare for the life I would live that no longer revolved around my sickness. *Who am I without it? What is my purpose? How do I keep myself in check without the staff monitoring me every day? Who's going to catch me when I fall down?* When I lapsed in treatment, I had endless support. The real world wasn't going to coddle me until I was ready to walk again. The real world would push me to the side to clear the walkway.

After insurance knocked me down, I knew to be successful outside of treatment meant I had to prepare myself for the world out there. I started small. I wrote positive messages on my mirror with expo markers, I hung out with only people who were supportive, I unfollowed triggering accounts on social media and stopped scrolling, I bought new pairs of shorts that fit my healthier body comfortably. I began setting goals for myself, I was looking for employment, I was setting up outpatient therapy, and I was working on my relationships with Noah and my family. I was trying to eat outside of treatment, not just in there. I vowed to always tell someone close to me if I was having a rough day instead of keeping it in like I used to.

I could not hide my struggles anymore because mental illness, especially eating disorders thrive in secrecy. When I was keeping it from my loved ones, there was no accountability. I could destroy myself in private and walk around looking perfectly fine to everyone else. I couldn't worry about disappointing Noah anymore. Telling him when I was having a rough time allowed him to fight for me when I didn't think I could fight for myself in that moment. Telling someone that I was working on a drinking problem would have helped my friends understand. Telling people didn't disappoint them, it just made them aware. It was a way to ask them to keep an eye on me. Having accountability added more reasons for me to keep fighting.

I believe everything about treatment is necessary to be able to have recovery from mental illness. Treatment was a safe place to fall, to break and to learn. But it's inevitable that we were unable to be sheltered forever. I began taking action on my goals.

My first major goal was to go sober for a weekend while still living my life. The weekend after the intervention, I chose to do as I normally would on a weekend and go along with the friend group. The only change I made to my plans was sobriety. I wanted to see how it went. At first I was feeling internal pressure to "just have a couple", but I pushed through it and learned a lot about myself.

I didn't need enhancement of substances to be liked. I learned that I could have fun without drinking, act goofy, dance around, and hangout with others who were drinking. My friends never pressured me to drink when I told them what I was trying.

After the first sober weekend, I had more weekends where I simply chose not to drink. I kept all my plans with friends, I just drank water or energy drinks. It was never about the alcohol, it was about needing to escape myself and please others. I had another eye opener that should have been obvious. Being drunk vs being sober didn't change the way my body actually looked.

The new way I started to view my life was totally different. I was actually looking forward to creating a life for myself, which naturally lifted my mood a little bit. Being nourished gave me more energy and the ability to hold a conversation or be fun. Because of those little things, I had the confidence to be sober that weekend which set the tone for the way I handled my weekends moving forward and still.

I could choose not to drink when I knew it wouldn't go well. I found moderation when I felt that drinking would be fine. I was able to stop after a few. I learned to stop in the middle of a crowded bar and listen to my body. A mindfulness skill I didn't know I had. I asked myself questions and felt out the situation around me. *Was I tipsy? Did I need water? Did I need to slow my pace? When was the last time I put food in my stomach?*

There was a time in my life where complete sobriety was my only option, and I didn't take it. Instead, I got worse, put myself in danger, and hurt those around me. I think complete sobriety is the answer for those who know that's best for them. I started with those few weeks of sobriety at a time because it felt less permanent. Because of recovery, I found that I didn't require alcohol to be good enough, I wasn't addicted, I didn't have to rely on it like I had before, so I didn't.

Another thing I needed to work on was building back up my relationships, especially with Noah. I was keeping him at a distance because I didn't know what he thought of treatment and mental illness. I had never just asked him what he thought. I had to start allowing him into this part of my life.

Every Tuesday evening was Family Night. That meant any family member could come to the treatment center for the last couple hours of the day. The first half of the evening was one big group session, everyone. There would be an activity that would later be discussed. Sometimes a short video or presentation by one of the Therapists followed by questions, answers, and conversation. Other times, a special guest (someone who had graduated from treatment and been successful in their recovery) would come to speak and take questions. The second half was dinner. We would all eat together, sitting at multiple big square tables. Parents and siblings eating with us too.

For a while I was one of the few that didn't have family come because mine lived 14 hours away by car. Noah was all I had nearby and I wasn't quite ready for him to attend. I was afraid of what he'd think. Plus it was nice not to feel the unspoken pressure from someone I loved in such a fragile area of my life.

I didn't want to disappoint him, but on the other hand, I also didn't want him to show up and think *She doesn't need to be here.* Because what if he saw me being successful during a meal and thought I milked my need for treatment? Or what if I disappoint him if he saw me struggling in there? What if when he sat in on the first half of the night, he thought it was all overreaction, or even bullshit? There was just too much unknown and I couldn't handle more conflict in my life. All I really told him was that treatment was good for me and I was doing my best in there.

Since my goal had been to allow Noah into this part of my life, I finally asked him if he wanted to come to Family Night. He was nervous. He didn't want to say the wrong thing, or get eye rolls for not knowing something basic about eating disorders. To be honest, that wasn't an irrational concern. Some parents would say stuff that was extremely insensitive or triggering and Noah had only heard those stories about family nights. He heard all about how we would all look over at each other, eyes wide. *Can you believe they just said that?* To be fair, it was only the parents who weren't willing to believe their child was sick. The insensitive ones trying to prove why their child is too large to have an eating disorder. The parents who refused to try to understand. Noah was neither of those. Once I convinced him of that, he started coming to Family Night close to every week.

He saw a lot. I think he learned as well. I asked him what his thoughts were about family night. He said it made him realize how big of a disease it was, how diverse it was, different sizes and genders, the different ways it affected individuals and families. Family nights opened his eyes to the world of eating disorders rather than just hearing about it from me. He saw it for himself. He said it was one thing hearing about it, but a whole other thing seeing it.

It's not that he never took my eating disorder seriously, but before attending family nights I felt like he got more frustrated with me as opposed to sympathetic for being this way. I think before he didn't have much context as to what I was going through, I came off stubborn, selfish, lazy, and unwilling to get better. He just wanted me to be better and didn't understand how much it took to get there.

I don't think it's easy to believe how bad a mental illness is, especially if you have never met anyone else or gone through it yourself. It sounds fake almost, or attention seeking. Like it should be easy to fix. I think a lot of people had a hard time grasping the intensity of mental illness, especially eating disorders.

Family night allowed Noah to see a bunch of other people struggling with the same thing as me. After a few family nights, he could feel the heaviness of mental illness. He sat surrounded by it, he listened to other people besides me speak about it, he listened to professionals speak about it, he witnessed the tears and mind games Ed put us through during dinner.

All of my peers and all of the staff at CFD loved Noah. They thought it was so sweet of him to come straight from work to family night. I remember we would all be sitting around the couches in the main area watching our families arrive through the giant windows. Every time Noah's red Colorado parked, my stomach fluttered and everyone would look at me and smile. When he walked in, they would all wave to him and make eyes at me about how cute we were together. Even the therapists would rave about him, how cute he was walking up in his work clothes, sharing a big comfy chair with me, and participating in the activities with me so intently. It was such a good feeling having him involved. I never should have doubted having him there.

Noah told me that before family night, he felt like he needed to be my caregiver when he really just wanted to be my boyfriend. We had been together for 3 to 4 years at that time and the better part of our relationship was spent dealing with my struggles. Fighting the darkness consumed so much of our time together. We still had good times, but he knew what was going on underneath my surface. Family nights allowed Noah and I to be more open with each other about the way mental illness has affected our relationship.

Something that has helped me a lot is feeling Noah's little way of confirming my permission to eat. Of course, I never needed permission, but in early days of recovery, he could give me the little nudge that took me off the fence. For example, I was finishing up eating and Noah had seen me having a battle inside my head. His response was "get seconds!" It was that simple. Instead of letting me battle it out in my head, his comment was permission to eat more. Sometimes Noah's voice was louder than Ed's voice. Before he would leave for work, he'd give me a kiss and say "eat your breakfast when you get up!" He would also rephrase it sometimes by asking what I was going to eat for breakfast. I knew I needed to, but having his voice side with mine against Ed was more powerful than just my own.

Another goal for the outside world was to work on my resume and start looking for jobs. I knew that in order for me to keep up with recovery, I needed to have a job that was meaningful to me. I would not and could not go back into the toxic food industry. I needed to feel that I had a purpose. I wasn't going to be easily replaceable anymore. The world was not going to eat me alive anymore. I wouldn't let it.

I volunteered at a place that I liked and had an interview on the spot. The next morning I got a call with an offer. Toward the end of my treatment experience, I was able to start part time and go to treatment part time. I became a direct support staff for adults with autism. I worked with them on social skills classes and activities, life skills tasks, vocational skills at actual job sites, and extracurricular activities throughout their day. We focused on independence, behavior, and integration into the community a lot. I loved working directly with the clients and building relationships with them.

As my hours at the treatment center were lessening, I was getting more hours at work. I was coming into treatment with a smile every time because I loved my new job.

The last thing I needed to do to prepare myself for the outside world was setting up my outpatient therapy. I needed to make sure I had a therapist to see once a week and a dietician to see every other week. I couldn't do recovery on my own. Outpatient therapy was going to be there to keep me in check. I went back to Melissa, the outpatient therapist I saw before treatment. I also went to an amazing dietician named Alice. I was ready to take on the world.

25

Guilt

It felt good to see the dreams I hid away before. The goals I set for myself while in treatment allowed me to be secure in that discharge would not leave me lost like it had before. I learned that I always needed to have something to work towards and look forward to in life. I found that having something to look forward to keeps my thoughts moving forward instead of back in the past. It gives me a sense of purpose and identity.

I was no longer working on just healing, but building myself to be the person I wanted to be. Hope is such a powerful thing. And with that I knew I couldn't expect to be the Michelle that I was before. I also knew I would never be capable of healing in the same place that held the pile of pieces I was broken into before treatment. The people I surrounded myself with, the environment, and my actions would be different this time. I set up my life to be worth something.

I knew I was ready because I was changing. I wasn't changing because I had to, I was changing because I was grateful. I was excited to become someone I wanted to be, ready to get more out of life. I wanted to live, not survive. I was not going to be the Michelle that entered treatment. I didn't owe her anything. I was going to be the Michelle I was always meant to be.

I was finally seeing the light that I didn't know existed. Depression, anorexia, OCD, alcohol abuse, trauma were all so tangled that I couldn't just tackle one, I had to tackling all of them in treatment. To do that, I had to start with one, and that was eating disorder behaviors. Then I was better able to work through the rest with a clearer mind. I had to nourish myself to flourish. In order to keep myself motivated during the rough days, I wrote a list of positive outcomes that came from nourishing. Sometimes I needed the reminder that I was doing the right thing. Here it is from my journal, written in 2019:

My hair is growing back and becoming thicker
Having more energy
Thinking more clearly
Better memory
I don't have to be worried about feeling weak or light-headed when standing
for extended periods of time.
My limbs don't fall asleep easily.
Tasting food again
I can be out in the sun without feeling like I'll pass out.
My family is less stressed
I'm less irritable
Noah and I are growing better together
I don't need alcohol to have a good time
I have motivation to do things other than sleep
I'm living toward values that are important to me
Having likes and dislikes. Finding out who I am.
Integrating hobbies back into my life
No longer dissociated, but fully engaged in the moment
My personality is starting to come out again.

I remember one day in treatment I was playing a board game with peers during a break. I used to isolate myself, but now I was playing with them and cracking jokes. Stan walked by and heard me. In passing, he said "She's back". I loved hearing that, I had a personality!

My discharge date was coming up fast. I had mixed emotions. I knew I was ready to graduate from the program, but it was still scary knowing I wouldn't be around my greatest support system anymore. On my last day, I wrote the staff a letter thanking them for helping me get my life back. After reading it to them, I started to cry because I was guilty. I felt undeserving of recovery. I wondered why so many other people suffering couldn't have healing and why I was one that could.

I thought about all the people more deserving than myself of healing. It's sad to think that people are out in the world suffering because they don't have insurance, or don't have other resources or support. It didn't help that *Sick Me* made a lot of mistakes. I didn't deserve good things when I compared myself to others. There were amazing people out there who never drove drunk, never put themselves into dangerous situations or sexual assault situations, were never dishonest or manipulative and never avoided family phone calls. They deserved recovery over me.

I left loved ones with scars. There were people affected by the things I went through, it was never just about me. My parents, Noah, my brother, and many more including JayJay, my pet bird. I adopted him in middle school, and he continues to be part of the family still to this day.

A therapist once told the group that people with eating disorders can unknowingly pass on some of their habits to pets. I overheard peers speaking about how they would never expose their animal to any of that. They seemed angry that anyone could do such a thing. I reflected on the life I gave JayJay and began to realize I wasn't far off from one of those horrible people.

When I was much younger, I took good care of him, but when taking care of myself became too hard, it was just as hard to take care of JayJay. There were times his seeds or water needed switched out and I waited longer than I should have to do so. His water got dirty fast because he liked to dip his food in it. I never left him without food or water, but I slacked a lot on keeping it fresh and cleaning his living space.

Without even realizing it, I was giving him the life I was giving myself. My room was messy and laundry didn't happen often. Sometimes I didn't shower, brush my teeth twice a day, or drink any water because I couldn't get out of bed after work. My depression and lack of motivation stretched to even the most innocent little creature. I thought I deserved to be neglected, but JayJay deserved better than that.

I felt like so much time was spent worrying and wondering about me that my brother didn't have much room to bring up anything he might have been going through. He was the introvert and I was the extravert. My presence seemed to overpower his anyway, and with the things I was going through, he stepped back even more.

Things like this weighed on me. Every time I started to feel good, I would remind myself of why I shouldn't be feeling good. I would shut it down because of my guilt. The therapists concluded that feeling good was overwhelming for me sometimes. I hadn't yet gotten used to having happy emotions. When I finally could feel that again, I was skeptical. Looking for the catch, looking for it all to crash down on me because I can't possibly deserve to feel this good. And if there was no catch, I was ashamed for having the privilege of feeling happy knowing so many people were still hurting.

26

Working Through the Trauma

I had a lot to work on with my outpatient team. I was doing really well when I was discharged, but I had to maintain it. I also had to continue to get even better, because by no means was I done. My outpatient therapist, Melissa, was the one I had seen before treatment but ran away as soon as she mentioned it. I assured her that I was there to stay this time and caught her up on my journey through recovery.

The first few sessions with her were just scratching the surface. Working through situations where I hadn't completed my meal plan. Brainstorming how to make a trip to the grocery store less anxiety provoking. Talking through a tough moment I had that week about my body in a swimsuit.

I kept it surface level for a while to prove to Melissa that I was doing great. I wanted her to take me seriously when I promised her I wasn't going to let myself fall back into the hole. I filled that hole back in, made it a garden, and destroyed the shovel. I didn't want her to think I just covered the hole with some flimsy wood planks like in 2017. I was in recovery, and there was no way I would let myself relapse again.

She could tell there was more going on than just with food. My depression was under control, but there was something holding me back. I had mentioned briefly about my guilt for recovery, but I never went far into that with her. I avoided thinking about or speaking about a specific part of my life. After the few easy sessions with her, I became visibly upset with shame. This time she pried. I told her I can't fully enjoy when good things happen to me. I was still feeling the guilt. One of my main reasons was the sexual assaults. Everything that happened after that moment was defined by that moment. The thoughts and memories of it tinted everything good.

The thing your mind tries hardest to avoid is often the thing you need most to talk about. I had to unpack what happened. It was eating me alive, but I couldn't get myself to tell the story out loud. I had opened up about it in treatment, but it was a very watered-down version. Melissa asked if I would rather write it down and bring it in the following week.

My story was folded into a tiny square that I brought to my next session. I sat and watched her eyes go back and forth reading every line of my story, placing her hand on her heart. The further down she read, the more her body language looked as if she gained the details of a shocking mystery. She looked up to see my eyes flooded. The first thing she did was apologize to me for having gone through that. I didn't understand. No one had ever apologized to me for something that was my fault. I refused to allow myself the comfort of considering myself a victim.

This session with Melissa would be the first time I really let myself feel the pain behind those specific memories. In the past, I would hold myself together. In treatment I sugar caoted it and left things out. In Melissa's office that day, I felt safe to let myself fall apart. I told her I would never believe her no matter how many times she told me it wasn't my fault and she accepted the challenge.

The topic of the assaults came up in every session from that day on. I was 25 years old when I learned what sexual assault meant. No class ever taught me that information. Not until the session, many months after the experiences, sitting across from Melissa is when I learned the definition of sexual assault. I wouldn't consider myself a feminist in terms of today's extreme version. I don't lean strongly in either direction when it comes down to modern day feminism, but I know when something isn't right. I find that in the subject of sexual harassment and assault, women's hands are tied.

The culture today has become so unphased. Everything is sexualized. It's been ingrained in our heads that sex is no big deal anymore. Much of the sexual harassment and sexual assault is swept under the rug because *it could have been worse. It's she should have known, She didn't do enough to stop it, Why was she walking alone? What was she wearing? Why did she drink so much around them? What did she do to give him the idea that he could?*

Those on the outside of a situation want to believe she could have prevented it. But in what world should a woman have to expect harassment or assault from anyone and everyone she surrounds herself with? It's always our responsibility to be on guard and take extra steps not to get taken advantage of. My reasoning for keeping my experience to myself was because I knew the reactions and opinions of society. I would have been cornered into more shame.

I feel like the whole blame of sexual assault starts with the simple things. The blame is placed on any small steppingstone that normally wouldn't matter, but because something happened one of those times, it now becomes the reason. The choice to go out is often where it starts. Then onto the clothing choice. Then onto the choice to drink. The moment the woman could have chosen differently, it falls on her. Should we not leave the house? Should we not dress nice? Are we all supposed to be sober? This is where we're cornered.

If I wear baggy clothing, I'm a slob, lazy, or not put together. If I wear something that looks nice or forms to my body better, I am judged on what my intentions are. I don't dress myself to be sexualized, I do it to boost my confidence. It feels good to get dolled up once in a while. I don't expect anyone not to look, but an outfit is not consent to touch me.

If I ignore a man that wants to talk, I'm a bitch. If I mention that I'm with someone and not interested in anything more, I'm self-centered and assuming. If I entertain a conversation because I believe there are nice people who don't have further intentions, I'm flirting. There is no way to win when someone comes up to talk. I'm either leading someone on or I'm being pretentious. I have always been the person that believes everyone is good until I have reason not to. It's disheartening to know I should be skeptical of any man who comes near me.

In recovery, I drink for the same reason any guy wants to drink while out. Social reasons, to let loose. It's dangerous for me to accidentally drink more than intended, but a funny story when a man does that. We all mess up sometimes when it comes to drinking, why should it only come down on women making that mistake?

Melissa taught me that nothing gives someone permission to touch you if there isn't an enthusiastic yes. Not a yes because you're scared, not a drunk yes, not a flirt, not a yes after feeling pressured to say it, not silence, but a clear, non-hesitant, yes. Nothing less.

Telling my whole story would mean enduring the questions from people who wouldn't know the feeling. I didn't want my story picked apart for answers in the things I did or didn't do. I didn't want to hear the opinions of people who had never been under someone they hadn't wanted to be under. I knew I didn't hold the answers they would be looking for. I didn't have the answers that would make me the perfect victim. I knew what the right answers were; that I tried fighting as hard as I could, or that I was drugged, that I kicked and screamed, that I immediately went to the police, that I never went back to work again. My answers were wrong. No one was going to understand me for the lack of reaction I had.

Melissa explained to me that even though fight or flight are the reactions we hear about most, there are two more. It's *Fight Flight Freeze and Please*. For many of my experiences, I froze. Sometimes I was so dissociated that I just couldn't get myself to react. Other times although I tried to fight it, I froze after the fact. I walked away like I had seen a ghost. I didn't tell anyone, I didn't cry, I just stared at nothing. A numbness that left me with nothing inside.

I was the character in the scary movie that makes all the wrong moves. The viewers yelling at the screen because what I should have done was obvious. Instead of running out of the haunted house with a weapon and yelling for help, I hid underneath a blanket inside the house hoping that would protect me from the monsters.

There are so many movies or shows that cause me to cringe at the characters' responses. It's amazing how much we think the reaction to something in the show is obvious, but the character doesn't do it. We want the woman who was abused by her boyfriend to leave, but she often doesn't. We think she would easily sneak away, find a place to stay, get a job to support herself and her kid, start a new life and never look back. It doesn't work that way. It never will be that easy to do what seems obvious.

Every session, I sat fiddling with balled up, soggy tissues while she told me it wasn't my fault. She kept saying there's no right or wrong way to handle it. She drilled that into my head. What I did or didn't do changes nothing about the fact that these things happened to me with no consent. Nor was my brain receiving nearly enough nutrients to be working properly. I barely had the capacity to process what was happening to me. I had given up on myself at the time. I was in this weird limbo between desperate helplessness and carelessly surrendering. I was an emotionless bystander to my life. I just thought I deserved what came at me.

I spent many hours praying God would lead me to the right way to handle my secret. I discussed with multiple therapists about whether it was best to tell Noah or spare Noah. No one ever gave me the answer, but often made me think more about what I wanted to do. Early one morning before work, I was in tears, calling our Pastor. I asked him what to do. I was so guilty for keeping it in, but I was scared it would scar him. I couldn't bear the idea of hurting Noah so deeply, putting a picture in his head that could be permanent. I wondered if I should just bear the guilt for the rest of my life and let him live a happy life without ever feeling that pain. Pastor Josh prayed over the phone for me and I left it up to God.

I worked through the hardest parts of my story for far over a year with Melissa. After 2 years, I finally got up the courage to tell Noah what happened to me. We cried together, we sat in silence together, I answered his many questions, and we worked through it together for a week.

Rightfully so, Noah questioned why I hadn't told him sooner. I knew he was trying not to be angry or doubtful. I told him honestly that I hadn't been ready to tell him until I worked through it myself. I didn't want to still be a broken mess about it while also trying to cope with his reactions. I knew they would be anger, hurt, and doubt. I had to be mentally stable, clear minded, and rational to help Noah through it. One of us needed to be healed from it enough to help the healing of the other. I needed his strength and positivity while I worked through it with Melissa first, and he needed my strength and reassurance while he worked through it later on.

I had always called it sexual assault until Noah said to me "You were raped. That's rape". Melissa also used that word, but told me I didn't have to say it like that if I didn't want to. I still don't really know exactly why I can't say it myself, but it is true. The heaviness of this word is attached to me whether I accept it or not.

27

Disconnected

Melissa also led a therapy group that I started going to. There were about 5 of us who had been in recovery from eating disorders and attended the group. I was still new to recovery, so some of the group topics had me emotional. There was one group where Melissa asked us all to close our eyes and listen to our body. There was a short meditation guiding us through the process of tuning into our body.

As soon as I started focusing in on myself, the tears immediately fell. I was nourishing my body, I was taking care of it now, but I still hadn't been in touch with it. I did what I knew was right for the sake of my mental health, but I avoided the connection between mind and body. Having been numb for so long, having been sexually assaulted, having been so hateful towards myself, I didn't really know how to love it or even like it for that matter. I was completely disconnected from it.

During the meditation, the voice told us to find out where in our body we feel tense, sore, comfortable, uncomfortable. It also walked us through relaxing all of our muscles from head to toe. That was horrible. I had avoided meditations for the exact reason of not wanting to put any focus on my body. In this I was forced to acknowledge the shell around me that carried me everywhere I went.

I was so reluctant to follow along, I kept peaking at the group to see if anyone else was feeling the way I did. When the voice started to tell us to hug ourselves and lightly put our hands on parts of us that needed comfort, it almost felt like an apology. I was realizing how terribly I treated my body. Realizing I neglected it for years when all it ever did was help keep me alive.

After the meditation, Melissa said she noticed a reaction from me and asked if I wanted to share. The group looked at me as if I was supposed to explain what had just happened in my head. At the time I only knew I hated meditations and the head to toe awareness stuff.

Everyone from group shared their experiences from the meditation, but Melissa seemed to think there was more than I was leading on. She brought it back to me. They told me it's normal for someone with an eating disorder to dissociate from their body. She talked about anorexia and the effect on the insula. She explained that the insula is what allows our brains to communicate with our bodies and vice versa. Often times, the insula in people with anorexia does not function properly. She said it was normal to freak out when we finally tune in after so long.

I hadn't really thought about it but being sexually assaulted added so much of the space between my mind and body. Melissa said something that clicked. *The line becomes blurred or even non-existent between what we know as safe touch and unsafe touch.* So many people had touched me without permission throughout my young adult life, and it blurred my lines severely. During the meditation, even my own hands made me feel uneasy. It felt wrong, inappropriate, and uncomfortable.

I started feeling bad for my body. Although I had been doing what was best for it, I hadn't quite acknowledged that it was part of me, it didn't feel like mine. My body kept going despite all the things I put it through. During my early days in treatment, I was given the assignment to write a letter to my body. I was still fully immersed in my Ed so the letter wasn't genuine. Because of the meditation and new mindset, I had decided to rewrite my letter when I got home. I wanted to mean what I wrote.

To my body,

I am truly sorry for everything I put you through. I never should have taken my depression out on you. You never did anything wrong. Thank you for fighting for me when I was neglecting you. I am thankful for my arms because I can hug people I love. I am thankful for my legs for taking me where I want to go. I am thankful for my stomach for holding and protecting the organs that keep me alive. I am thankful for my face because I can share emotions and moments with others without words. I promise to treat you the way you deserve to be treated and to practice self-compassion. You never need to change in order to please others, and I now know that so I will protect you. Because of you, I will take many adventures. From now on I will try my hardest to fight for you when my eating disorder gets mean. I'm on your team. You are such a great friend to me and deserve to be taken care of the way you took care of me.

Love, Michelle

Sometimes I come across old pictures of myself and they bring up mixed emotions. I look beyond the smile, location, or way I looked. I feel the heaviness of the time, the ugliness of what I was hiding, the pain I was carrying, the emptiness in my stomach. It's hard to look at myself smiling back then and think back to what I was dealing with underneath. In some pictures I can specifically remember what was going through my head. In some I can remember it was taken before I got trashed and blacked out. Some I can just remember the loneliness and depression I was feeling in that moment. Others I can remember the struggle in the mirror of self-hate and outfit changes before picking the outfit I wore that day.

Seeing pictures of me before recovery makes me sad for that girl in them. She had no idea the damage that was still ahead of her. I grieve her missed opportunities to live free of mental illness. I want to tell her she has a future and it's brighter. I want to protect her, take her to treatment right then, no waiting, no suffering in secret. I want to hug her and tell her she deserves to take up space in this world, and to start fighting for herself. It's hard to look back and grieve all of the things I could have done right, experiences I could have enjoyed, and nights out I could have remembered.

My path may have looked different than others, but it brought me to where I am today and I am thankful for that.

28

All of the Moving Parts

One evening when Noah's parents had come to visit us, we went out to eat. My taste buds still weren't finding food very tasty, but it was the first time during recovery that I was able to taste the food in the way it was meant to be. I was so excited that I told everyone at the table even though it probably didn't make a lot of sense. I was hungry for it, I actually enjoyed it, I didn't have to force anything. That gave me hope that the more I nourished myself, the more I would be able to enjoy food again. It was the start of an even better recovery.

My appetite for food slowly creeped back in after the dinner with Noah's Parents. That moment was a good wave of momentum, but it was only one of the many moving parts of maintaining recovery. Depending on the day, if one moving part lacked, the rest could be thrown off completely. My Mind was a complicated web of these moving parts, all working together to make sure I could stay in recovery. Sometimes I over complicated it, sometimes I didn't do enough, sometimes I forgot, sometimes I thought I was good to recover without trying.

There are many times my mind gets scrambled when it comes to maintenance. It's frustrating, but I have the tools to fix it, I just have to use them. Sometimes I think these things only happen to me, but when I confide in friends from treatment, I find out it's not just me. So everyone can see they're not the only ones, I wrote a little bit about the weird, little things that come up sometimes.

I have to be extra mindful when life situations heighten my emotions. Whether something makes me anxious, mad, or even excited, my appetite often doesn't align with my hunger. At this point in my recovery, I am fully aware that I need to nourish and I'm willing to comply. Although my hunger cues have mostly come back, there are times they go missing and eating feels more like a chore. Sometimes I'm hungry, but my appetite for any food at all is gone.

I came from a place where the pain and guilt of eating wasn't worth recovery. Now my voice can drown all that out because recovery is more important to me than Ed's empty promises. I get upset with myself when I fail to follow my meal plan, but sometimes I'm the reason it didn't happen. Any good or bad heightened emotions can make me forget to eat or listen to my body, take away my appetite, or psych myself out when I think too much about what I need to do.

When I put pressure on myself to eat, I think too much, trying to plan out how I'm going to do it. I make myself anxious and then my appetite is gone. I put too much focus and planning on myself, so nothing sounds good or easy to eat. When I force myself to eat something that I normally would enjoy, I feel the way I did in treatment. Forcing bites, trying to keep it down. Maybe it's the OCD, but my mind remembers the physical struggle I had with that specific food in that moment, so for weeks afterwards, I am repulsed by it. Because of my association of that food and the physical struggle, I take a while to ease myself back into having it again. That's just one example of the way Ed can come in and scramble my mind.

Hunger cues and appetite aligning is a big goal for me, but it's not everything. I paired pleasure with shame for years, even in recovery. At some point in my life, I started to become embarrassed to eat in front of others. I thought of a video online someone showed me with this dude who ate anything. He would eat insane objects or dangerous amounts of real food or alcohol he was dared to devour. I had to turn away because I got grossed out and quite honestly scared for him. He was shoveling food (or non-food) into his mouth, the only sounds of the video were chewing, breathing, and swallowing. I couldn't stand the sounds either. I compared myself to that guy when enjoying food.

In high school, I would go to my friends' basketball game and then out to eat with them. I hated eating in front of them, especially being that they were guys and I didn't want them to have a gross image of me. I remember trying to wait until their attention was on something in the other direction so I could take a bite or two. I would make it really quick. I never took bites when they were facing my way. I was terrified of seeming gross, or of someone asking me a question when my mouth was full. Sometimes there wouldn't be enough chances for me to take a bite that I didn't get to eat enough even though I wanted to. I'd be wanting to eat more so bad. I would leave the restaurant hungry, just to keep people from judging me.

Another time in high school I had been going on dates with someone, but I remember our 2nd or 3rd date he wanted to take me to eat somewhere. I can't explain the anxiety of waiting for that date. I dreaded it. I made all these plans in my head about what I could order that wouldn't be hard to eat nicely. I had hoped he would use the restroom at some point so I could scarf it down while he was gone. I was terrified of eating in front of him.

After treatment, I was still feeling shame for enjoying food. But I couldn't let that keep me from eating like it had in the past. I had to relearn eating in social situations. I had to eat at a normal pace, take bigger bites, have what sounded good, not what was least shameful. I realized that I felt bad for enjoying something that so many people are trained to avoid, good food. But I was stronger than Ed and I was equipped to handle the task. I was not that dude on the internet. Nor did I ever eat with anyone who seemed like that guy. It was all in my head, if no one else ate like internet guy, then I didn't either.

I was honest with my dietician about my fear and shame. We talked through it a lot, but she wanted to take a bigger step. She wanted our next session to be at a restaurant and we would eat while having our session. She said she'd order the same thing I ordered to make it easier. I immediately shut that down. Each session she would offer that to me again and I couldn't accepted it.

I would camouflage myself at work during lunch time. I avoided sitting across from coworkers. I would walk around with my lunch and eat it as I paced so I didn't have to sit and have a conversation with food in my mouth. I could turn my back to my coworkers every time I took a bite. Part of me felt embarrassed and rude for eating, even when everyone around me was doing the same thing.

One day at work, I had trouble eating my lunch because there was a lot going on and I was overstimulated. I had to keep getting up to help clients, there was a lot of noise and an incident with an aggressive client as well. That day I had my lunch in a circular container. From then on I never put my lunch in that container. Whatever was inside that container would automatically send my mind to the feeling of my struggle to eat.

My eating disorder snuck through every tiny hole that it could, putting these associations together, adding fear and shame. It doesn't go away, but it becomes easier to quiet and quicker to dismiss.

29

The Final Pieces

I had three items I couldn't get rid of for some reason. These three things were physical items left of my eating disorder. I didn't use them, but I wasn't ready to let them go.

The first was a specific pair of shorts. This pair of shorts fit me when I was sick and actively using behaviors. I hadn't tried to wear them since before treatment. They were in the top drawer of my dresser, easy to find, but I knew they wouldn't fit the same or maybe at all for that matter. Even with knowledge that I would be upset trying to wear them, I also couldn't get myself to give them away. It was a little bit selfish because part of me thought if they didn't fit me well, I didn't want them to fit anyone else. Letting go was like letting go of the fact that I could ever fit in them comfortably again.

The second thing I wouldn't let go of were my diet pills. I hadn't taken them since treatment, but something about never having them again was scary. I knew I wouldn't use them since I was at a good maintenance stage in recovery, but I still needed to know they were around.

The third thing was my gym membership. I felt like to be a legitimate person in today's society, I had to be a member of some kind of gym. I would look around and see people being praised for going to the gym, talking about their workouts, checking their daily steps, calories and all the things. Next to conversations about the weather, working out felt like a close second to most popular topics. How would I be a real person if I didn't at least workout once in a while? How would I be worthy of conversing with if I wasn't at least a member of something fitness.

Today's media pushes us by preaching that going to the gym is a staple to living a productive and successful life. It had been months, maybe a year since I had gone to the gym. I was wasting 20 dollars a month for it and canceling was choosing not to go back ever again.

The gym was a trigger. I knew I would never be able to go into a gym and be kind to my body. I knew I would never be able to work out moderately in that atmosphere. I knew I would be triggered by every well-toned woman in there. But having the membership meant I could maybe, possibly still go someday and get that high I used to feel. I missed the feeling.

My eating disorder lived with me for so long, and even though I didn't want to fall back into it, I was afraid to fully part from it. Ed had fully encompassed my identity before, and I was still finding out who I was without it. These items were just reminders of my past identity. I was still holding on.

After a few months, I was ready to part with one of them. I handed my diet pills to Noah, walked away, and told him to do what he wanted with them. I knew he would get rid of them somehow, but I also didn't want to be there for it or know about it. I asked him months later and he told me he flushed them down the toilet when I wasn't home, and I never missed them again.

I still have the shorts, but they're no longer in the top drawer of my dresser to remind me each time I open it. They're hidden in the back of my closet. I may not be ready to part with them, but I don't think about trying to fit into them anymore. They're just there.

Almost a year after flushing the pills, I was ready to cancel my gym membership. By this time, I wasn't stopping myself from canceling, the gym was. All the hoops I had to jump through just to cancel it were impossible. I tried five different ways of cancelling and when going in person to cancel didn't work, I shut down my bank account and set up a new one. It really opened my eyes to how these places get people stuck.

30

We Forget How to Play

I met with Alice for sessions every other week. She always made so much sense. Other than being my dietician and making sure I was doing what I needed to do, she made sense of every mystery I brought to her. Every little thing I wondered about, she had a factual and clear response. She explained why I need body fat in each area, what it does for me, and why it's important. She explained why every single person needs Carbs, Fats, Protein, and Fruits/Vegetables. She debunked every fad diet with solid facts and broke down all my concerns.

She worked on a movement plan for me since I was restoring my body of its nutrients. This meant I was allowed to safely ease into physical activity again. She called it Joyful movement, not working out. I could pick something I would enjoy, but not punish myself with. Going to the gym was not an option, I knew it never would be. I wanted to try playing tennis again because I used to love it. She allowed me to play for an hour per week if I ate an extra snack each time. After a few weeks, she would reassess to see if I could add more time.

I was excited to try tennis until it set in when I got home. I felt hesitation. What was wrong with me? Why didn't I feel like grabbing my racket? I was given the opportunity to pick up a hobby I once loved more than any. It was placed in the palm of my hand, and I didn't take it. Something wasn't right. I just couldn't get myself to go when I finally had permission to play again. I was afraid, not excited. I was afraid of failure

I thought back to the effect mental illness had on my love for tennis. Two weeks later Alice asked how tennis went. I told her I didn't play. We processed the most recent memories of tennis that I had. Before, when I loved it, I was healthy and well-practiced, but most recently, I played when

I was sick. Those were the times that my passion started to fade. My eating disorder took the fun out of it.

I couldn't play for as long. I was malnourished and weak, my energy was completely drained. I was tired just from a few hits. It got to the point that walking to the courts tired me out too much. I would try hitting around with Noah and my arms just felt like noodles. I would hit the ball into the net and get so angry at myself that I'd shut down and ruin the whole mood. I couldn't laugh off my mistakes like I used to. The more frustrated I got at myself, the worse I played. I would throw my racket at the fence, cursing at myself. When I was in it, there was no fixing it, I was angry and done. I couldn't hit anything in that mindset. The feeling was terrible. It wasn't fun anymore when my eating disorder came with me to the court.

I had a fear of failing like that again. I was afraid of finding out that tennis was permanently ruined for me when I wanted so badly to love it again. I figured I would have some energy back, but not the skills. I didn't want to get frustrated, I just wanted to be decent at it. What if I would never enjoy playing unless I was hitting well? Self-compassion was not my strong suit, and I knew I would need it. I also imagined I was out of shape and wouldn't be able to do much. Tennis was a lot of running and I hadn't really run in a couple years. I hated the possibility that I would never have fun playing tennis again.

Three years. I put off my easily achievable dream for 3 years after I was given permission to play. I thought about it all the time. It was the anticipation of disappointment that kept me from grabbing what was placed in my hand. I lived next to a tennis court for all that time, my rackets were in plain sight of the garage. I had two brand new, unopened cans of tennis balls sitting next to the rackets. Every time I saw them, I ached for a good play. I'd get frustrated with myself. I had to rip the band aid off. For three years I left my rackets untouched, begging me to play.

No one is born with an innate need to conform or change. It's learned. It's learned through the insecurities created in us by society and media. Sadly, it seems life is no longer about having a purpose or making a difference, but about reaching an impossible standard for an invisible club that's defined by comparison. We feel we need to be approved of by others.

So much of our energy goes into striving to be enough. Mentally ill or not, we are all consumed by the negativity created around us.

When it came to food as a child, I ate when I was hungry, I ate what sounded good, and I stopped when I was full. It was intuitive. Because I never restricted cookies, I didn't crave cookies all the time. Because I allowed myself to be satiated, I never felt temptation to binge. So many adults would be happier in this world if intuitive eating was as desirable as fad diets. The human body is incredible. When it tells us something, we ought to listen.

Fad diets want us to ignore our body's needs. Disordered is now desirable. Dieting is now self-discipline or even self-care. If we all fed ourselves the way our bodies are meant to be fed, we wouldn't need all this keto, fasting, juice cleans, 30 day diet junk. These programs don't care about your health, but only about our insecurities paying their bills. It's all about shedding pounds with no regard for the damage it could cause in our bodies. We talked a lot in treatment about what happens internally that diet programs leave out.

These industries say they're trying to fix us, but they don't want us to feel better. They want us to constantly think we should be better. They want us to beg them for solutions to fix ourselves when they created the "problem" in the first place. And whatever it is we're doing will never be enough. There will always be more we could be doing or buying to become closer to enough. It doesn't end.

When someone loses weight in a way that's not meant for our bodies to go through, they're congratulated and praised. Someone who doesn't go to the gym to workout can be seen as unmotivated or even lazy. It's so backwards sometimes when the ones hurting themselves are congratulated and the ones living life intuitively are looked down on.

Imagine being congratulated for skipping dinner out with friends because you were on a diet, missing 2 more hours a day with your kids because you had to go to the gym after work, spending money on diet pills instead of a good book, studying weight loss online instead of doing hobbies. Imagine being congratulated for missing out because your mind was elsewhere, focused on not eating the cupcake at some party, comparing yourself to the other people there, guilty for cutting your gym time short to make it there. Imagine being congratulated for being irritable with your family because you're hungry and the salads you've been eating for dinner don't give you what you need. Imagine being congratulated for depriving yourself of basic needs. Is the number on the scale worth it?

If only we all could go back to a child's mindset. When I was a kid, we played. We were accidentally active. We did what was fun, exercise wasn't punishment, looks didn't matter. There were no thoughts about calories, appearance, sets, reps and numbers. It was simply playing around the neighborhood, climbing trees, riding bikes, tag, kickball. There was no pressure. We were too innocent and without screens to distract us from what really mattered.

I'm sure no one wants their child to fall victim to the culture social media has created. It's toxic, it's taking mindfulness out of moments, and taking comparison to a dangerous level. Social media has made it clear that appearance is the priority over values and personality. It's shallow. And I'm here to tell you, this lifestyle takes everything out of you. We, as human beings deserve better. We forget to take a step back from the screens to smell the roses.

We become so engraved by the message that looks define our worth. We're wrapped up in working hard to change our appearance instead of exercise that boosts our mood and keeps our bodies strong and healthy. In treatment I thought I missed going to the gym so much. I thought I used to love it and be so motivated to go. One day in Alice's office during a conversation, I got quiet and said "I just realized I don't actually like 'working out' and I never did." I thought I missed it but what I missed was the validation it made me feel. The approval of societal norms. The measurable way of keeping track and doing better.

Some people actually enjoy going to the gym, and God love whoever you are. But that day in Alice's office I decided that all it ever was for me was punishment to my body. A chore. I didn't need to put myself through that if I didn't like it. I didn't need to quantify everything I did, treating my body as a to do list.

I'm active in ways that don't feel like a chore. Fun things. Noah and I do all kinds of active things that aren't intended for change. We are always out walking around, swimming, riding bikes, attempting to roller skate, dancing. I'm always on my feet at work. It doesn't trigger me anymore when Noah goes to the gym because I know his intentions are strength and a happy body. We have a good balance of active versus rest in our lives.

Before, when I was immersed in the damaging world that called itself "health and wellness", I didn't leave much room for anything else. I was always preoccupied, lending my head space to these disordered thoughts. The life path I was on started to point toward the wrong things, leaving behind the path of experiencing, learning, doing, and being. It's much harder to enjoy life while simultaneously trying to keep up with all the rules and expectations of appearance.

When I was growing up my mom had said something that stuck with me. She was worried about people coming over because, in her words, our house wasn't immaculate like theirs was. She talked about how beautiful and nicely furnished their houses were. She ended up coming to a realization that I really respected. She said our house may not be as freshly nice as theirs, but it's lived in. Our house is lived in. I loved that.

We had fun in that house. Games and toys were still on shelves instead of vases and China plates. We built forts, we jumped on the couches, we sledded down the staircase, it wasn't just a house, it was our home. It wasn't messy or dirty, it was nice, we took good care of it. But having an immaculate home was not realistic in order to truly live in it.

It was the experiences we had in that house that made it so memorable, not how nice it was or how new everything was. Imagine looking back and wishing you had done more than just push yourself too hard for something that doesn't matter in the end.

When I think of the way we all try so hard to be perfect, especially on the outside, it takes away from the more important things in life. Our bodies are not to be a showcase for others, but to be lived in. The body in which we are living our lives, doing fun things, present in the moment, is the body we are meant to have. Not one who is focused on being perfect, starving, unable to enjoy the moment for what it is. We're not here on this beautiful Earth to be preoccupied with a bunch of crap, we're here for a greater purpose. An immaculate body isn't worth the years of missing out on the gifts life holds. It's the bodies lived in that have the fullest lives.

31

Breaking the Seal

For a long time, I thought to enjoy something, I had to be good at it. I thought I had to be good at tennis to even step foot on the court. And of course, there was the fear of tennis being ruined forever. Three and a half years after graduating treatment, four and a half years since I last played, I finally took the chance.

It was a beautiful day in January 2023. Too cold to get in the pool, but too nice not to enjoy the outside. It was 75 degrees and sunny, Noah and I were still on Christmas break from our jobs, and we had no plans. I silently debated with myself the whole time we ate breakfast. Finally, I just asked. *Should we play tennis today?* I knew Noah was down, but I knew he didn't realize how big of a deal this would be for me.

I explained to him all of my fears, how nervous I was to find out if my favorite sport could make a comeback for happy and healthy me. We went over to the park, I took a deep breath of grace, and I hit the ball with an exhale. The weight of my fear was lifted as easily as the ball went over the net. We didn't play any matches, I asked just to hit back and forth, letting go of any measurable aspect.

I gained a lot that day from picking up my racket and facing my fear. I gained a peace of mind, tennis was fun again and I didn't have to be great to enjoy it. I could laugh at my mistakes again, give myself kindness and grace in those moments. I felt free from the pressure and anger that once ruined the passion of the sport. And my energy matched my game. I didn't become a spaghetti noodle after a few minutes.

To Noah, it was just another day, but to me it was a breakthrough. It wasn't about finding out I wasn't as bad as I thought I'd be, it was about the feeling. I couldn't stop talking about the feeling of getting back out there, I spent the rest of the day on that high. No weights, machines, or numbers needed for this high. The hardest part was over, and I was ready to integrate tennis back into my life.

My other favorite hobbies that I had to bring back were painting and drawing. My last few paintings went unfinished because I gave up. I was a perfectionist and becoming more depressed at the time. Art began to stress me out too much instead of the other way around. I just wanted everything to look exactly like I pictured. Before getting sick I had all this inspiration, seeing in my head what I wanted to create on the canvas. When I got sick, I had no ideas. I would stare at a blank page trying too hard. It wasn't fun anymore.

I began painting again in 2020, a year after I graduated from treatment. All I did was start painting one picture with no expectations. I broke the seal and regained my passion for art. There was no need to be perfect at it, I took any expectations out of the equation and just went for it. Whenever I started to get anxious about how it would look, I reminded myself I could paint over it. If it was bad enough, I had other canvases to start over. That was the secret. It didn't need to be a complicated process to get back into.

32

Meant to Be

In the decision I made to honor my body, I learned more about the things that were truly important to me. I no longer looked outward for my purpose in life. I trusted that my purpose was within myself. I continued to maintain my recovery, which brought to light the things I was meant to do. I felt called to serve individuals with special needs. And I was healthy enough to do so.

The job I started at the end of treatment was the job I worked for 3 years before my dreams grew further. It was a day program for individuals with autism, behavior based, where we worked with these individuals to improve their quality of life. For my first year I worked mostly in the adult program.

We would take them out into the community to do fun things. We would take them to a job site where they got to work on vocational skills with our assistance. Sometimes it was at a restaurant, the YMCA, the bowling alley, etc. We worked with them on life skills and social skills. We did fun activities and games with them. We took them to the workout room at our facility To work on gross motor skills, we had music class once a week, and my personal favorite, art class once a week. Each client had specific goals that were personal to their level of functioning. We got to help them work on achieving those goals. They ranged anywhere from matching colors, learning the alphabet, how to write, respond to a peer in conversation, or even some academic goals.

Sick me was not confident in herself, she was afraid to take on responsibility. The difference was clear when I was no longer sick. At this job, I was confident in what I was doing. I was confident in the way I handled client behaviors. When the opportunity to have more responsibility was presented, I took it and I wasn't scared, I was eager. I became a leader and example for others.

I started up the art program for the adults. Every Tuesday I had an art project or lesson set up and ready. I taught the class, I brought in the supplies, I even asked for a display shelf in the front lobby to show off their art. Before, I never would have had the confidence or energy to start something new. Never in a million years did I think I would be bold enough to ask the founder to put money into something that I wanted to do, but I trusted myself and I saw value in what I was doing.

Another part of my day was working in the recreation program. This was working with children with special needs at the same center. There was an afterschool program and camp in the summer. I moved up to the Lead position of the recreation department. I never would have been able to keep up with the demands of this job had I not been in recovery.

Instead of stepping back during a crisis, I jumped in and did what I learned to do. Before, when a client got aggressive, I would take it personally and overthink it. There were many times that a client would need to be safely removed from an area or safely restrained when they became a danger to others or themselves with high magnitude behaviors. Because I was properly nourished, I had the mental and physical strength to assist in those situations and even take charge.

Old me would have been scared to get too close, healthy me doesn't bat an eye, jumps in, and follows the procedures without hesitation. I'd come home from work with bruises, bite marks, spit in my hair, or scratches with a smile on my face because I got to see the difference I could make in a situation. People don't always understand why I am so in love with what I do. For me I love the relationships with clients. I see myself grow in those challenging moments as well as seeing the clients grow. Whether it be that I was able to get the client to bounce back and rejoin the group, to calm someone down, redirect and prevent a behavior, or having a major breakthrough with a difficult client, I lived for those small victories.

Because my mind and body were no longer sick, I became a strong staff member that was trusted to handle many things. I was designated to train new staff as well. I gained confidence in handling tough situations. I liked working with difficult clients. I was assertive enough to share ideas and suggestions with the admin.

I enjoyed teaching social skills or life skills, I lived to watch them improve. Art class was just as fun for me as it was for them. I got to show these individuals that they could make beautiful art. After three years and some soul searching, my dreams had me reaching further out. I am now a teaching assistant at a school for autism and hope to keep growing. I don't know exactly where my end goal is, but I'm following the passion and I trust that it will all work out. None of this would be possible without recovery.

Recovery gave me so many reasons to live. Everything Noah and I went through made us stronger than ever. Because of our darkest moments, we learned how to work through anything together. We got through the destruction of mental illness, and the times of our relationship where we were hanging by a thread. The beauty of that was the way we learned in those moments, grew emotionally, taught each other, and became pros at effective communication. Because we suffered so deeply, we now have an incredible love and support for each other. The foundation is unbreakable.

Noah asked me to marry him at our favorite beach. I had no idea he had my friend Kristal come, and my brother and two cousins fly in from Ohio. When he knelt down to ask, they came running out from hiding to surprise me and we spent the weekend with them. It was so special.

Wedding planning was surprisingly so much fun. I was confident that no mental illness would be invited to our wedding. I wouldn't let it take any space in the process. My eating disorder didn't come with me when I tried on dresses, my anxiety didn't sit with me leading up to the day, and depression wasn't even close. I didn't need alcohol, I had a few drinks throughout the whole night, but I was having so much fun that I'd leave my drink somewhere and forget all about it. I never once cared about getting more. I remember how relaxed I was the day of the wedding, and recovery was to thank for that.

Marrying Noah was the best thing I have ever done and nothing could have stopped the positivity I felt that day. We love our life here in Florida. We adopted a cat that we named Crunchy. We fixed up our home to be colorful and fun. We survived the lockdowns of covid without once getting tired of each other. He lets me paint murals on the walls in our house, we found a church to call home, and we have such great friends surrounding us. I'm amazed every day at our blessings.

33

Blessed

Recovery will never be a destination, it's the way I live my life and always will. I have ups, I definitely still have downs. I always will. I lapse, but I'm aware when I do. I can fix it and use my support system and coping skills. Recovery is making myself get back on track. It's making sure I am not battling alone, because that's where the opportunity comes for mental illness to grab me by the ankles and pull me under. Recovery is taking my medicine consistently every day as prescribed, whether I want to or not. I know this helps me and the difference is significant. Recovery is waking up and choosing recovery every single day.

In the past, I hadn't told people when I was having a hard time, that's when the demons came out. They could pull me too far, and by the time I tried to speak, my voice was muffled or gone. In 2019, I had to promise myself to be honest with at least one person when I'm struggling. I need accountability, and in harder times, I cannot always hold myself accountable. I can convince myself all I want that I'll get through without having to disappoint or worry a loved one. Maybe that's true many of the times. But the one time my lapse becomes a relapse, I'll know I was silent. I'll know that no one was aware to help me before I got that far.

In a maintained recovery, you fall over, and you're aware because you go from a good place to a place that hurts. You can either cover it up or ask for help. Let someone in, maybe they'll help you up, maybe they'll just be around if you need a hand. Don't hide it. Some day when you fall, if it's too hard to pick yourself up, you'll need that hand. Without accountability, it can become easier to stay down than to try getting up on your own.

It doesn't hurt as much to fall even further when you're already down. It's not as noticeable if the spiral has already been in motion. When I was falling, it was easier to go back to my eating disorder than to work hard for recovery.I heard once that holding onto something that's too easy to hold, when held too long can destroy you.

Promise yourself, always let someone know if you're having a hard time. It's better to say *Today I am fragile, I may need an extra push* than to spare someone that small moment of concern, and later cry out from a place too deep to be helped. You may not see your worth, but someone else does. People want to be there for you. Let them.

...

We have all asked at some point why we suffer. Why does God allow suffering? What is the purpose? I think there are many purposes, but there are a few that spoke to me specifically through my own experiences.

Through suffering, I learned. I became more empathetic. We are all sinners, we all do things that aren't right, but through our own suffering and sinning we gain understanding for each other. I think of how it's not my place to judge because I don't know what's on someone's heart. I became much more aware of the way I thought about other people who made mistakes. Who am I to judge or comment on someone's choices when I don't know the circumstances?

I gained ways to connect to anyone, to meet people where they're at. God met me where I was at during my worst moments. I learned everyone deserves that grace. God doesn't seek out the righteous, he seeks out those who fall short so he can move through them.

Through my suffering I gained a voice, the skills I have today and the drive to help others overcome the fight. While suffering, I learned who the people are that will stick by me through anything, the people I want to surround myself with. Through my suffering I learned what really matters and I figured out who I am.

Back in treatment 2017, we were asked to write what we thought recovery would be. I didn't care to do this activity, so I just wrote a word. *Freedom.* When I wrote it, I hadn't really believed it. I was just following a prompt. I can picture the way I wrote freedom with a shrug, having no idea it ever could be that good. I was stuck in a windowless space that never allowed me to see what was beyond its border.

All along, freedom was the perfect word to describe it. Recovery is freedom. It's going from surviving to living, being free from the prison in my head, from the expectations of society, and from my past. I climbed out of the walls that held me and my past hostage, and I stepped into the present. I shed my old coat and I walked much lighter, exploring the world free from the heaviness.

I thank God for his mercy and grace while I struggled. I fell short in many ways. I stopped praying when I was sick, questioning if He even cared. I destroyed the body He made me by cutting and denying it of basic needs. I drank to black out. I was reckless. I put people in danger by driving under the influence. I was the all-time least perfect victim of sexual assault. I lied to friends and family all the time about how I was really doing. I avoided phone calls from them. I lived by shallow values instead of what I knew deep down was right. But God still provided.

There's a little story of a woman talking to God. He had walked with her through life. There were always two sets of footprints in the sand. One day she looked back and asked God why when she needed him most there was only one set of footprints. God told her It was then that He carried her. I had been oblivious to the fact that He carried me through the worst parts of my life until I could walk on my own again. All this time I thought He called only those who were ready for him, but He doesn't call the equipped, He equips the called. I was meant to come out of this.

I made so many mistakes, yet He still loved me. Why did I deserve his grace and mercy? I grew up learning that God forgives us of our sins when we come to him, but I needed more. It still didn't make sense. It felt rehearsed to say that, to make Christians repent. How could God actually forgive everything we've done? I was searching for answers through therapy, but my answer came from a typical Sunday in church service a year into my recovery. *God knows the heart.* That was my answer, made clear as day.

He doesn't keep tabs on specific things we've done, he surpasses those surface level things and looks straight to our hearts. Although I had made mistakes and distanced myself from him, God saw what was on my heart. Despite my actions or lack of actions, even when I didn't know who I was, God knew who I was. My heart revealed my intentions, my true values, my struggles, and my deepest feelings. He knew that I was protecting myself the only way I knew how. I longed for a relationship with God again, but I didn't know how. He knew that and restored me where I fell short.

I thank God for the blessings he put in place of my illness. In every prayer, I ask for continued motivation so I can keep living this life as the Michelle I was meant to be. I know what I'm fighting for, and I know how to fight for it. Most of all, I know the fight is worth it.